v v v

This
Uncommon
Place

v v v

Forward

As poets, we pay different attention to things around us than non-poets might. This unique perspective lets us glimpse profound moments of artistic beauty, but can also have an isolating influence. To see the river is not to be in the river. The lesson I've learned after years of sometimes-difficult experience is that a story is more exciting from inside than from the outside. Through living deeply we can create great poetry, though it's harder (and sometimes more painful) to see the details when you are so close to them.

Kevin Watt, editor

Table of Contents

Virginia Hahn - How dare you...tiger   1

Lisa F. Raines - And I'm not gonna make it home   3

Perry Bach - Cold Season   4

Tim Pare - Love and Kissing   6

Patricia LeDuc - Diamond Rain   11

Laurie Grommett - Mangotango Minneiska Apple   12

Marilyn Griffin - I am the desert wind   14

Roger E. Miller - Hull 54, where are you   16

Philip Jenkins - The Second Ice Age   18

Ann Copland - Renaissance Sky   20

Bomo Albert-Oguara - Themes from the Sunday Pew   22

Bomo Albert-Oguara - Themes Part 2   24

Nancy E. Jackson - Cokes and Creamsicles   26

Adam Hebda - Crystallization   28

Ann Copland - Flowers and Ice   30

Bomo Albert-Oguara - Southern Kada   32

Keith W. Gorman - My Childhood Toys   34

Paula Gliot - Harbor Hideaway   35

Adam Hebda - Aeolian Conversations   36

Steven Visintainer - A Setting for Hay   38

Ann Copland - Everybody has a Bathroom Skip to:
Constitution Ave. Loo   40

Lisa F. Raines - Knights in White Satin   43

Howard Manser - Slapdash Fellows at the Shambles Saloon 44

Marilyn Griffin - the single couch   46

Lisa F. Raines - Get out of your head   48

Laurie Grommett - A Golden Boutonniere   49

Howard Manser - Adrift   50

Melissa Davilio - Prismatic Feathers Falling   53

Jozef Neumann - Planes and buzzards   54

Alwyn Barddylbach - Dreamcatcher   56

Mary C. Galindo - The Claim of Heritage   60

Jozef Neumann - motorcycles   62

Nancy May - Start Continent   63

Lorri Ventura - A Bostonian   64

Douglas Pinchen - The Pith Helmet   66

Gavin Brosche - A Hard Town for Poets   68

Mary Scattergood - Granny's Brown House   73

Beverley Wilcock - Renewal   74

David I Mayerhoff - In A Foreign Land   76

Arlice W. Davenport - The Light of Love   78

Jenny Middleton - Forget-Me-Nots   80

Robert Buck - The Iron Gate   81

Marilyn Griffin - Surfing with sharks   83

Juan Pablo Segovia - Do not cry for me   85

Carl Wayne Jent - Harvest   87

Joseph Phillip De Marco - The Most Sacred Voyage   89

Krishna V Ramavat - Spring on Sand   91

Kenny Reeves - I remember   93

David I Mayerhoff - The Unforgotten Night   95

Joseph Phillip De Marco - The Zoo   97

Ashantae L Stone - Autumn   98

Daniel Duna - Petal Jumpers   99

Rueneta Barclay - In The 1800s   100

Madeleine McLaughlin - The Snowball Fight   102

Michael Fuller - Grand dad's box   103

David I Mayerhoff - A Perfect Evening   104

Kylie Jensen - One red shoe   106

Joshua Appleby - finding   108

Tobias Bang Søgaard - White Lilies   110

Kayla Nakabasa - Bhutan's Majesty 111

Richard Fairchild - Spanish Sun-glow 112

Janet Paulin - Spider in my Shower 114

Kimberly McNeil - Birth 116

Hannah Lipman - Gratitude 117

Ashwini Kumar Rath - Saint of Woolsthorpe 118

Gilda Math - African Landscape Musings 119

Carolyn Caudle Castle - Adventure With Pokey 120

Dylan Clark - The breeze 121

Ian Lee - Consternation and Constellations 122

Jennifer Randall - Hanka at Ninety-Five 124

Florence Elizabeth Samples - A Winter's Call 125

Lisa F. Raines - Rainy morning - Wouldn't you know it 126

Sandra Poindexter - My first injection administration 127

Kiana ModoLowe - Black or White 130

Mary Elizabeth Vanorskie - Some Dim Light to Work By 132

Christopher A. Patrick - Autumn's Beauty 133

Emeli Dion - One Planet to Call Home 134

Lisa F. Raines - Take Me Home 136

Ann Copland - Lady in a Bar 138

Kathryn Kass - The Shaman's Rattle 140

Deborah F. Thomas - The Immigrant 142

Patricia LeDuc - A Sweet Summer Day 144

Katharine L. Sparrow - For the Love of Bob 145

Samantha Kriese - Thawing Hearts 148

Ina J Evans - Tiles mock runways 149

Christina Marie Cuevas - Not looking back 150

Lisa F. Raines - Betrayal 151

Paricia LeDuc - All Is Well For Me Today 152

Laura Gallagher - Mirror Mirror 153

Gabrielle Antoinette - "The Poetic Act" 154

Peter Boadry - There was a Donkey Named Dave 155

Stephanie C. Keeley - Parisa and the Pantry 156

Douglas Pinchen - The Men from 1894 Tolpuddle 158

Swaytha Sasidharan - Poetry and Me! 159

Lisa F. Raines - Even if It's All of the Time 160

Mirza Lachinov - The worst poet to be punished 162

Misha Jane Berry - White Demon 164

Katarina Anne - Goodnight Universe 165

Ina J Evans - My prize, your flesh 166

Carlos Vargas - Stardust 168

April Hamlin- Sache - Angel 170

Stephan V. Mastison - Goddess 171

Saad Ali - Immortality 172

Lisa F. Raines - Quiet my fears, show me the lies 174

Phillip Davis - CAW CAW, missing feather 175

Lisa F. Raines - The Stench of War 176

Nitya Beriwal - Theory of everything 178

Kristopher Burnett - Broken 180

Anna Mortis - I've been gone a while 181

Benita Hall - Would You Have Regrets 182

Juan Pablo Segovia - A place in time 184

Marri Rouse - Magic Sand 185

Lisa F. Raines - He is my heart 186

Kristyan Wilson - Is it or is it not Divine destiny 188

Michael Cruce - Peace for us, Peace For life, Peace for all,
Peace for love 190

Lenard Carter - In the Final Hour 192

Juan Pablo Segovia - An old friend 200

Lisa F. Raines - Foolosophy 202

Juan Pablo Segovia - A fallen tree 203

Robert Scott Henry - Repeat 204

Alex Crowcroft - The Enlightened State Of Mind   206

Jack L. Martin - Sit Down, Shut Up and Listen!   208

Kathryn Alley - Beyond the Pale   211

Arlice W. Davenport - Anguish   214

Laura Gallagher - Liberate Yourself   215

Marielle Diala - Sought after   216

Rhonda Barringer - Grandparents   218

Peter Witt - Notes from Cell Wall   220

Michelle R Sass - Emotions   222

Lisa F. Raines - You Disappointed Me Today   224

Rebecca Brodzenski - You choke on pysch pills   225

Lindsey Johnson - No Longer Dependent   227

Patricia LeDuc - Another Time, Another Place   228

Jenny Linsel - The Birthday Party   230

Lisa F. Raines - Headphones, really?   236

[Virginia Hahn]

How dare you...tiger

how dare you, tiger, freely roam
where jungle orchids crown your home
your burning sinews never rest
O fearsome queen of wilderness

how dare you plunge into desire
and taste the mysteries of your fire
your incandescence flashes might
o tiger in the wildest night

O clawless tiger in a cage
with lacquered poles and jerks of rage
you're slowly snuffed by man's damp heat
his porn and plastic at your feet

it's you he worships, you he'll kill
his iron jaws and clenching will
you're forced into the prophet's mould
for meds and margins, guns and gold

O tiger in our darkest night
we're meshed in existential plight
we dare to smother your orange light
O queen of all that's wild and right

[Lisa F. Raines]

And I'm not gonna make it home

Why do I want to go home,
when you're not there anymore?

Why do I say goodbye every day,
when I wish you were here?

Why do I cry, try, dry my eyes,
deny my cries, decry my life?

Fight, flight, slight light, always right;
Lie, lie, lie, lie, lie, lie, LIE

AlisRamie is from North Carolina, USA.
Interests include: philosophy, history, international relations,
poetry, art, design, jazz, funk, and some good old soul.
Allpoetry.com/AlisRamie

[Perry Bach]

Cold Season

I've been a recluse this stormy season
Sleet batters my face, the west wind howls,
And the white pure flakes of Christmas
They've drifted and darkened like my heart

Love's been so cold this winter season
I speak delusion and white lies to my mirror
I've turned my back to north winds and true friends
Feel darkness slither thru my door

And I long for peace and warmth of Canaan
The land where milk and honey flow.
I've been trekking for forty years of winter desert
Light me a candle as I'm surely heading home

Waiting for a blessed and gentle springtime
But I've scattered good seed among the weed and thorns
I can't turn from old ways and cold rain
Chill and danger still lurking at my door

I'll be filled and burning bright come springtime
Gentle rains wash pollution from my soul
Dormant love will blossom as the snow melts
Surely sunlight brighten up my door

Yes, how I long for sunny days in Canaan
Where the milk and honey forever flow
Done trekking circles thru life's wasteland
Burn warm oil till I find my way back home

Hopesummer52 is from Twin Cites MN. I form lyrics and melodies in my head while running. I've written over fifty pieces since 2018. Allpoetry.com/Hopesummer52

[Tim Pare]

Love and Kissing

Truth is, it's in my face.
Like flesh with its pinching-baby's-cheeks elusive quality
And I've been searching for it all my life.
Standing in a dream now with memories of Nadine,
and Kathy, and my sis,
them waiting for the instructs on the passion of boys.
Nadine said, "looook! This is how it's done!
Come here boy, close your eyes."
But I never did. I stood looking shy
into that beauty that men vision,
the dream state of tongue-open
and a French kiss of a vision
Nadine went frost.
All frosty in gray flannel pajamas
like the stuff of grownup seeds
and grown men
like passion flowers
the midst of May,
the mist of Forget-me-nots.
I just opened wide for that.
I stood wild-in me, and smiled
smiled, smiled at the wet of her.
She liked me. I was cool.
Kathy was the frightened one.
I was 10 she was 14.

Her kiss was like a hot
shower. Too wet from nervousness,
and too long.
My god, she never got it right.
Like long goodbyes,
she kissed me again and again.
I was a sad boy, all trimmed and proper
to then. I'd never kissed, touched dreams.
But the one, my mum, like truth.
I dreamed early, like a sick cow
giving birth.
Like my home
the barn was hot,
and too dry, too small
my legs cramped often.
my house was, "shh shhhh" quiet.
quiet like church-mice,
library prayers
A house of gables and suspended
In the middle by attrition, stimulation
I looked up; I was wet from sweat
a child's dream.
I was lying in a big bed. fluffy,
like hot rice-warm,
and the sweet smell of that illusive grace,
like candy, like ballroom dancing, like learning
to walk. You put him at an end and say,
"here baby, right here,
oh, right there, you can do it for mommy!"

And then, the waking, the waking in dreams
once, and once, and once, and...
Once I can't remember how long. it was before the falling
and failing and chastened chasing dreams,
chased, by who-knows
I woke, on soft rice, just before I was thinking:
loud hits, scores, long runs to second base dreams
ocean dreams of float-boats, invisible to eyes, and patience,
I'm going a long way
I woke just then on soft rice
and mum was there, not feeding other eggs,
Mum made me eggs all the time,
did I mention that?
she loved eggs and fed me cold.
it was my prayer that she feed me, even cold.
I laughed, woke laughing, and just looked up at
mum; no face, no eyes,
like canvas cover dreaming back
and a light, like the light now in my sky
centered in me with smiles.
How do I see smiles with no faces?

Kathy was like licorice.
forbidden in my house
because it stains teeth. Just that -
forbidden, like child-dreams of adult love,
like the saliva taste,
better, bitter, just eat whole,
shells and all, appetites

like hers didn't come till late in life,
to be first in a kissing-line,
make wet like nobody's business
and just kiss. Nadine knew.
No people asking, no explaining,
she just smiled at Kathy, red-faced wonder,
breasts sloping to an angle of me,
not pointing I was on the floor
anywhere, just firm like resolve
with a back just a little rounded in embarrassment.
Nadine laughed like hell,
and so did I.
She pointed to the door.
And I pointed with laughing eyes.
"Out boy, we're finished!"
What a wonderful dream. I can still taste it.

Kathy worked at a grocery store last time I saw.
and she smiled that big toothy smile, and said,
"Boy, you grew up!"
my god, her beauty haunts me,
her laughs and kisses
pulled me to those days.
I've never spoken these love-truths
out loud. Lately grace nudges the mind of me.
Me, I just listen like this day
when beauty scars and scares me
like frightened joy

like truth flash flesh and light
like beauty coming from the sky.

───────────────

I live in Toronto. Allpoetry.com/MichaelPare-Reid

[Patricia LeDuc]

Diamond Rain

Behind the majestic maple tree
The sky changes to gray
I hear the deep rumbling warning
From thunder not far away
There is a thickness in the air
A sign it's coming your way
The rain arrives
But to my surprise
When the rain stops
A beauty of nature
Sparkling on the pine tree you see
Little droplets of rain diamonds

———————————

Poetry is a creative way to clear my mind and put my thoughts into words. Mother/Grandmother/Happily Retired. I live in Middletown, Connecticut Allpoetry.com/Patricia_LeDuc

[Laurie Grommett]

Mangotango Minneiska Apple

As a viewer to a carjacking
for extra parts,
I stood backtracking
on prior recognitions;
you left me moonwalking
and stole the last whit
from my sun, whole.

In a jackrolling,
the gang acts as a boomerang
trolling top to bottom (wound wrenching),
but you played as a pillaging
pieceworker, tearjerker,
I laid as broken jewelwing,
a damselfly caught
falling from the blue sky.

The sweetango with the mango crisp
no longer juicy as rosy apple,
(plucked and f-cked),
I clung to dung ground
when my pit replanted
in a browned field,
reared by a jackleg, jiggleworm,
jumping bullfrog.

Piecemealing it back together
stood a minneiska apple tree;
I'm a crossbreed,
mutated, weathered
with a mix of sea-salt in the soil.

Laurie Grommett is a teacher that runs her own business; she
believes learning is for life. Her poetry also spans the gamut of
genres: humorous, fantastical, haunting, but always comes from
within. Allpoetry.com/L.G.

[Marilyn Griffin]

I am the desert wind

Below the purple crags of the
southwestern desert,
impoverished basins of river beds
long desiccated,
I inhale the four corners of
the red clay canyon

and in measured breath exhale;

find me giggling in the limestone
and in the cholla-
flinging barbs and teasing
the wrens' nests

with gentle fingers ruffling
through chest feathers of
pinkish blush,
while she in blinking rush,
her black eyes on skies,
churrups a shrill warning

and I
in tumbling through
her tall sanctuary of monstrosa walls
gather seeds of generations
and blow

gusting through the veins of the sun,
I skirt the dust
like a skipping stone
tugging a swirl of reds
from an autumn that
remembers

I begin as a gentle friend

Marilyn is a mother of two daughters and a grandmother to one perfect three and a half year old boy. She loves words and writes them down in little notebooks she keeps in her purse. Allpoetry.com/Greeningofautumn

[Roger E. Miller]

Hull 54, where are you

God has spared this old spar
chips in the varnish near the ends
but still weatherproof and water resistant
the sail's foot is secured to it
with braided cords of hemp
gnarled and twisted
looking like the veins in the back of his hands
running through brass grommets
eyelets crimped into doubled canvas
showing stretch marks
radiating out like crow's-feet

a little sag in the body
but firm at the corners
good for another offing

sail ho
haul that anchor, boys
pull it like ya want to have a hernia
let out the jib
go below
put the kids in the crib

this week end
wanting to sail 'round the Horn
but sailing to Annapolis instead

trying to make it
out of this Baltimore harbor
and head south

such is not so
i am grounded in Michigan
a salt without savor
our Allied Sea Wind ll
hull #54
is out there, though
you go girl
sails full
cut those rolling waves apart
lean into the swells
make the anchor feel useless...
and fly

———————————

I am 'freewit' from Michigan. We were prepping our boat the
Lilac Maiden for blue water sailing, but better fortune was with
us when we received the opportunity to adopt two young
children. Bye bye, Atlantic waters. Allpoetry.com/freewit

[Philip Jenkins]

The Second Ice Age

The sun, once a star in the sky, now lies dormant in the heavens
circling the earth.
Our spring is now choked by frost and snow.
Flakes of white from heaven's east wind cast a fiery chill over what
was once green.

Man pumped iron next to the gods in clouds, in white clouds the
hour the first flakes fell.
For England in all its pomp and glory. Withered
as green giants vanquished all that lay before them,
handed over the crown of which once enthroned.
Over the seas the Putin monster from who's
mouth. Spate poison didst come.
Kremlin tv is knocking on my door.
For black loss shalt cover your fields,
Shepherds unable to count their loss,
Where is your July morn,
To where is your sunrise?
Eastern winds will only rise to frozen fields you will awake.
Pray take the winters. Chill that the earth may be kissed in
Warmth again.
The migrating wheatear and the sand martins plight as insects lay,
dead to winters bite.
How the raven's nest is covered in white,
Cometh the second ice age to plague this land.

Wait for the raven eggs to hatch,
then and only then will summer call.

I'm Philip Jenkins I am 57, born in Neath South Wales, currently living in Ashford Surrey, and have been writing poetry for the past three years. I hope you enjoy my work.
Allpoetry.com/A_year_or_a_day

[Ann Copland]
Renaissance Sky

Sunny Highway 16
through Central Mississippi
a stop light at Carthage
miles of shade .

Forty five minutes
from the airport.
Thirty two acres
of sovereign land.

As one drives up the
last hill, out of the trees
in the midst of vast... nothing
rises a shining Golden Moon
to the North, on the South
glares a flashing Silver Star.

Neon illusion - a temporary galaxy
for travelers who arrive on buses, vans,
expensive cars, pickup trucks.

Controlled atmosphere   cold   weightless wealth
--- most held by illusionary gravitation
coins and cash stays, letting the vehicles depart.

A hundred million dollars
planted on the dusty planet
of Pearl River, Choctaw Indian reservation.

The Chief promised the Moon
and brought the Stars,
winning his Renaissance gamble.

Ann Copland lives in Virginia, looking for the good in everyone
and every day. Retired from government work, friends and
movies missed over the last thirty five years are her entertainment.
Allpoetry.com/Ann_Copland

[Bomo Albert-Oguara]

Themes from the Sunday Pew

dark the clouds hang;
ripe the fruits on tree dangle,
but would not descend
into the sky's pale yellow hue;

the boom, loud sound
of approach doom;
weak-kneed the hand-chain
to the gallows row.

the shepherd sweeps
our ebb and flow
towards the waving zealots,
swimmers dipping emotions low

army-worms beat path the road
trodden, against prevalent winds;
the sails flutter and flutter;
tatters flung into grass grain of dust.

chirrups of sparrow rises sleepy dawn,
while the cock's crow rouses lazy morn;
the home coming hunter sounds the mourn
dawn gong; aye! aye! the welcome party song

Bomo Albert-Oguara is from the Southern coast state of Bayelsa,Nigeria,a writer,who cherishes his art in poetry,my way of speaking in colors,on a varying range of topics private,but mostly public . Allpoetry.com/Bomo_Albert-Ogua

[Bomo Albert-Oguara]

Themes from the Sunday Pew- Part 2

loud lungs are mere tassels
that decorate the night
wafting through stuffed stifling air
of aged dogmas-
symphonic falsettos they wring
in our ears
rather silence remonstrates
from silent-land comes our rescue

brief our romance with blue skies
comes to naught
as night clouds race across the sun peep
through the slit a cocky smile plays round his lips
the wry look on the face of the moon
gives away the morning news
silent-land claims the precious one

but what oft repeated sights the herdsmen
ought keep their cattle closer to their stalls
not roam fields their yield to munch and gulp
then shriek the peace of the homestead
rage following the village beauties violated
to the sound of muskets slung and reprisals
rather silence remonstrates
the precious one among the catacombs lone

knots of conspiring braids round power
turns the oars of state to a nation of shallow rudder
cleft power shifts in conclave night.

Bomo Albert-Oguara is from the Southern coast state of Bayelsa, Nigeria, a writer,who cherishes his art in poetry, my way of speaking in colors, on a varying range of topics private, but mostly public . Allpoetry.com/Bomo_Albert-Ogua

[Nancy E. Jackson]

Cokes and Creamsicles

I half-stretch, half-skip to mate
my steps with his sweeping strides,
only my gawky limbs are poky -

his six-foot gait outpaces me;
falling behind, I trot alongside while
he ambles through our quiet neighborhood -

we walk silently on trimmed sidewalks,
inhaling scents of our sweat mingled
with newly mown lawns -

he glances from side to side,
puffing on a menthol
and clinching my tiny hand -

crossing the street toward the one-pump
gas station, we head for the red and silver
cooler just outside the tiny office -

Daddy pops the top off a frosty bottle
of coke and unwraps a Creamsicle; we take
our delights and relax on the curbstone -

his half smile reveals his mirth
over seeing my ice-cream melt sticky
on the front of my sleeveless shirt -

while I grin and
savor this time -

just Daddy and me.

Nancy grew up on a peninsula by calm and thrashing waters. She lives near foothills of blue smoke; her yards are havens for wild birds. Poetry gives voice to the world inside and outside of her. Allpoetry.com/Nancy_daisygirl

[Adam Hebda]

Crystallization

Meteors for her will fall
like crumbling walls of dominos
Rocks in rows the sky installed
explode in fire meadows

Shallow breezes blowing aerosol
strip the frequency from telephones
Vehement callow cat calls are
evaded by the dial tone

Melting algid oceans
will guide rivers as they overflow
Flaming comets flood the continents
into archipelagos

Fossils form beside her
and corrosion lined the reservoirs
She paints galvanic eyeliner
to freeze the fourth dimension guards

Her viscous focus quiets notes
to stall them in each measure
Silence broke the melomania
she soaked with saturated noise

Seal hydraulic envelopes
by pascal tons of pressure
and mail her letters to andromeda
welded to an asteroid

Falling satellites ignite
when sparked within the mesosphere
The sun will cease to rise in twilight
swallowed by a burnt horizon

Ashes fill the biosphere
and glisten in her rear-view-mirror
surrounding all in a tephra fog
until the planet disappears

Someday archaeologists
that sift the dirt and dust
will find fragments of her meteorites
crystallized to diamonds

I was born in the rolling hills of Tn, but my job as a tower climber has allowed me to traverse this beautiful country from a perspective most won't see in a lifetime. I am truly blessed. For Mel. Allpoetry.com/OutOfTimeMan03

[Ann Copland]

Flowers and Ice

vintage 1950's hand crank steel
ice crusher -
screwed to the wall, like it should be;
force behind your arm in the leverage
as you push the handle
the sound --
a deliberate crunch
non apologetic,
like chewing shredded wheat,
just under the intolerable pitch of chalk on a chalk board-
second and third grind and slice,
ice   fills the   plastic torpedo bottom
one yank frees it

scent of mint
Bourbon, taste of sugar,
hold the cup at the rim,
silver frost

civilized conversation,
three of us on the brick patio
sitting upon color coordinated, cushioned,
white iron furniture
surrounded by green and fragrant garden:

confederate jasmine flowering white,

bright St. John's roses,

yellow and purple snapdragons,

perfectly pink iris shading the mint

little blue flowers and tall daisy-like stems

a sight worth allergic nose itching,

I envy those who stay,

those who will enjoy blooms

yet to open

in the secluded summer garden.

Ann Copland lives in Virginia, looking for the good in everyone and every day. Retired from government work, friends and movies missed over the last thirty five years are her entertainment. Allpoetry.com/Ann_Copland

[Bomo Albert-Oguara]

Southern Kada

gloom is feisty this harmatan morning; eerie,
goska, kataf, kobin, the valley of the dead;
after violent thunder storm of hooves passed
through, war songs: "allah hakba! allah hakba! allah hakba!;

of a thousand calves, to their spears slain,
the hundreds innocent; to sun and rain exposed;
their flesh the ravens pick bare; grave fields of men,
women, young, old, even dogs and poultry unforgotten,

as a grieve-stricken two year old clings
to mother's dead blood soaked breasts;
i am grieved; this grief I feel for the rolling hills
of green goska, kataf and kobin;

like sponge the earth soaks the crimson flood
from the many slain; they, of "unworthy burial", none,
the rites to perform, the performers lay dead
beside the still flow of the river kada.

who shall then bury the slain of goska?
who shall then bury the slain of kataf?
who shall then bury the slain of kobin?
who shall ring the remembrance bells?

to those who slept the last sleep?
when all are cleansed?
who shall atone for goska?
who shall atone for kataf?
who shall atone for kobin?

when the cat bays the mouse of southern kada?
"Ku Kashe Arna" (Kill the pagans)
"Ku kashe Arna" (Kill the pagans);
war song of a thousand angry calves.

_____

Bomo Albert-Oguara is from the Southern coast state of
Bayelsa,Nigeria,a writer,who cherishes his art in poetry,my way of
speaking in colors,on a varying range of topics private,but mostly
public . Allpoetry.com/Bomo_Albert-Ogua

[Keith W. Gorman]

My Childhood Toys

Near the edge of my old school,
all of my childhood toys lie
bulldozed in a landfill.

Deep in the damp red clay earth,
roots of old mimosa trees
push the torsos of plastic men,

turning them as I once did:
their arms and legs locked
in a never-ending battle.

For over fifty years,
mimosa branches have leaned over
the grassy ground, forming a headstone,

splintering the noonday sun
into fractals of slow-dancing shapes;
illuminating the dust and pollen

suspended in shafts of yellow light,
just as I remember, shining golden
through the windows of my childhood home.

Savageheart is a factory worker from the Great Smokey Mountain
region of Tennessee. He loves hiking, biking and poetry.
Allpoetry.com/Savageheart

[Paula Gliot]

Harbor Hideaway

sun set along the Seashore
no Clouds to obscure the moonlight
lazy Dog asleep on a fishing Boat
docked in the harbor

local Tavern opens its doors
regulars descend like Vampires for tankers of ale
shucked Oysters laid out for the taking
all manner of Nyctophiles congregate

neighborhood Women scoff at the clientele
judging equally the drunken Dentist, Undertaker, sailor
all roughnecks and rebel rousers alike
all destined for the Graveyard before their time

but for those patrons who raise a glass
the inn brings comfort and laughter
comradely with friends and neighbors
a chance to kiss the day farewell

Paula (aka Katdream) is from Palatine, IL. Writing has been a lifelong process for me. It recently helped me through a battle with cancer by keeping me focused on hope and healing. Allpoetry.com/Katdream

[Adam Hebda]

Aeolian Conversations

Winds like howling wild coyotes
chastise incandescent skies
with moonlit chants of misanthropy
baying breezes bark replies

Whips will crack through granite stone
and carve between ravine chasms
Canyon walls erupt in echoes
quavering tempest decrees

Dancing leafs from auburn trees
convene beside a busy street
scratching sidewalks surface clean
from zephyr anthems spiraling

Gem stone sand on shores will glisten
rendering reflective tides
Gale force siren songs are tempting
tanker ships to sea floor's side

Prevailing tepid ocean breezes confess
their tormented cyclone anxiousness
Westerlien waves crescendo to their crest
and digress algid current's stark addresses

Heaven shackles to swaying chandeliers
blown by scintillating solar wind plasma
welded by fusion to the star's atmosphere
each corona a magnetic field of jasmine

Forces that govern all life will speak through each of us in a very
personal way, we are all pieces of the universe experiencing itself. I
write so I can learn from myself, and ultimately this force.
Allpoetry.com/OutOfTimeMan03

[Steven Visintainer]

A Setting for Hay

Day lights from stone homes
that began ten generations of family

here the ninth is woken by the rooster's call.
They begin their walk to ancestral pastures
amidst the burning of logs -
the terrestrial perfume of the alpine village.

Passing the seasoned wood piles along homes,
the graffiti noting births and crumbling facades
the family attends to their summer pilgrimage.
The fetor of sunned compost rises in wells
and mixes with the village's wood perfume
while on the dirt-paved road
hardened by foot and hoof
the dust still mists from the labor of their walk.
The edge of road meets land and across its slopes
allows the glance of the glow of the wildflower's rapture.

The trail births alps from its horizon.
The meadow now close, grown and prepped of stone
awaits the work of the household -
bronzed men and head-scarved women

to murder the grass and herb
and paint the human machine's back liquid beneath the valley
sun.

Birds here that cross the plain are finch and crow.
Woods frame the scene - pine, spruce, mingling beech.
Now, on the angled steep ground they work
sliced pasture -
the signs of the scythe's rhythmic sweep.

———————————

Steven Visintainer was born in Brooklyn, New York and raised in
Ridgewood, Queens. He has taught high school English in the
New York City Public School System since 1998.
Allpoetry.com/StevenNY

[Ann Copland]

Everybody has a Bathroom

Skip to: Constitution Ave. Loo

Blue jeans, beer,
gray open suit coats,
peanuts, parties
in the West Wing.

After the election:
red power ties, jelly beans
and a movie star's house
on his Hill.

Third floor Caucus Room
at the cross halls of history,
hearings and hospitality.

Our conference room
turned-holding-room
for First Ladies.

Adjoining government issued bathroom:
pictures hanging upside down for humor;
an odd book case turned on its side;
now

40

guest powder room with towels we don't use;
an end table with candles and flowers;
a toilet lid installed.

Transformation, courtesy
the gentility and personal expense
of our in-house
Miss Southern Hospitality,
who chased us away.
Secret Service swept
with dogs.

Decor followed suite:
Nancy Reagan red, Barbara Bush blue.
Once we spent a lovely hour
with Mrs. Carter.
Color scheme and flowers
adjusted for a lady named Rosalyn.

Probably I should have taken this early cue --
I might be in the wrong place.

My Really Pink boudoir is yellow
wait -- there's more, and green
(the one bath in our house).
I'm happy if there is toilet paper
and I don't step in water.
Guests use paper towels

ripped off a holder screwed to the wall.

Please, use anything you see;
try to dry the floor.

Teenage and twenty-something
artists, musicians, jocks, thespians,
students, working young men, sometimes girls
visit my green/yellow horror.
As if they were eight year old Cub Scouts,
I still pray for a flush every time.

Blue jeans, beer,
t-shirts and sweaters,
parties on my deck.
Conversation
every bit as interesting as
I'd find on Constitution Avenue.

The bullies in D.C. may have control,
but there is a better America.
Ask the ladies in line for the loo.

––––––––––––––––

Ann lives in Northern Virginia. She writes humor and reflection
based in memoir. Teachers of the National Writing Project
critiqued and guided her early work.
Allpoetry.com/Ann_Copland

[Lisa F. Raines]

Knights in White Satin

Never trying to feel
Just as our love is
We both must be real

Scary men out there
Burning the cross
Yet how will we be
Bracing for loss

Inhumanity haunts us
Robes red with reflection
Stalking each furtive kiss
Hate blinds the connection

And I love you
Oh, how I love you
Change the hearts of men
Please, God, show us how

AlisRamie is from North Carolina, USA.
Interests include: philosophy, history, international relations,
poetry, art, design, jazz, funk, and some good old soul.
Allpoetry.com/AlisRamie

[Howard Manser]

Slapdash Fellows at the Shambles Saloon

in the city of York, an English town
odd old buildings of russet brown
surround damp streets of cobblestone
pathways finding the party zone

jesters strike around half past noon
slapdash fellas crash the shambles saloon
with a splish splash, they dab a bath
the last stop on their dead-beat path

zag scalawags like to rally
at a mish-mash mosh pit sally
peaking the patter of jibber-jabber
through chit-chat and blasé blabber

the tip-top flip-flop clip clap crowd
are to the man vocally self-endowed
their tight tongues tied in a tangle
wag with rhythmic jingle jangle

hip hop beats on the radio
shadow rhythms entwine in stereo
with tic toc crisscross tapping toes
lift a cadence from depths below

when two pass noon at the shambles saloon
the characters mirror a black cartoon
days pass and quietly echo
dark portraits show tin art deco

Poetry is self-revelation. I am a son, brother, husband, father, veteran, and poet hailing from the historic Golden Isles of Georgia. I write my verse inspired by the seaside
Allpoetry.com/ProseAndCons

[Marilyn Griffin]

the single couch

on Tuesday,
the fractured windows
of the stores I passed-
spiderwebbing above
the sidewalk that blurred
like an Afremov painting

a black neon laser crusader's port

my motocycle boots
tromped with my legs still attached
exploding from hinged knees
in a march
past the furniture store

with an axe
when we, last Monday,
split all the tables and couches
in two

with my bloodied calf
from a table leg misfired
when you stripped us of all
we had

but the lust
of cutting things

with sharp tools and flinging
carved statues against the walls
then loping their noses off

till we
whittled it all down to shavings

and we fell
engulfed
in our tattoos

and the rain
thundered down

_____

A thank you to Kevin and the IPC for all your support on my poems. I am grateful for your encouragement! I just sit here and type. Allpoetry.com/Greeningofautumn

[Lisa F. Raines]

Get out of your head

My husband said
As I tried to turn down
his volume.

Another time,
as he reminds,
I tried to change the channel.

Don't look at me
like I'm so funny,
a character on your TV!

I need you to be serious now,
wake up and
see reality!

AlisRamie is from North Carolina, USA.
Interests include: philosophy, history, international relations,
poetry, art, design, jazz, funk, and some good old soul.
Allpoetry.com/AlisRamie

[Laurie Grommett]

A Golden Boutonniere

From pocketful of clear blue sky
reflection moves an autumn day
as amber honey leaves fly by
in golden boutonniere bouquet.

The lake-cast shadow from the trees
of shirty bronze and saffron bands
and cooling air shoots feathered breeze
across once greening timber land.

It smells of country sassafras
but english style with dressy mulch,
the surface of this looking glass
is streaming into narrow gulch.

A side of spice lays at the face
of weekenders led in, astray,
while tourists, trekkers, off the pace
embrace this october holiday.

Laurie Grommett is a teacher that runs her own business; she
believes learning is for life. Her poetry also spans the gamut of
genres: humorous, fantastical, haunting, but it always comes from
within. Allpoetry.com/L.G.

[Howard Manser]

Adrift

rootless on sapphire seas
tides dishonored then begrimed
a keel eroded, relentlessly thinned
barnacles disguised with time

drifting toward dark horizons
battered and barely alive
distant isles beg an appearance
pleading I arrive

beyond the rotting corpses
mired and run aground
anchored in the muddy depths
the Sea of Despair surrounds

fire-ravaged rigging
scared by flame and age
fail to bear the sails
billowing before winds of rage

salt-breached stores
neglect to nourish my
bloated belly filled with spoils
hunger pangs defy

lost upon the derelict
to no port do I belong

barren brown sandy isles
without an oasis or scarcely more
countless swells deftly erode
a deceptive sandy shore

dreams once charted a treasure map
leading me to distant virgin coasts
linger now in the swirling mist
reflecting fading failing ghosts

flailing from the yardarm
I beg reprieve once more
in the distance lays the land
of a milk and honey shore

riding waves of swirling crimson
on churning deep blue azure seas
surrender not to marauders
pirates or itinerant thieves

blues swirl destroying dreams
hurricanes batter weakening beams
darkness reflects in fractured mirrors
as blues drift through sapphire seas

Poetry is self-revelation. I am a son, brother, husband, father, veteran, and poet hailing from the historic Golden Isles of Georgia. I write my verse inspired by the seaside.
Allpoetry.com/ProseAndCons

[Melissa Davilio]

Prismatic Feathers Falling

Myriad colors flaring
like trumpets, strident, blaring
from painted maple leaves
vibrant as the setting sun

Crimson, umber and citrine,
magenta, coral, tangerine
clinging to outstretched branches,
dangling until at last they disengage

Tumbling in the Autumn breeze,
swirling like prismatic feathers,
draping the ground
just like a sweater
knitted from variegated yarn

Melissa lives in Bristol, CT, USA, and resides with her husband Jim and their furry family. She recently published her first book of poetry, entitled Earth Tones. Allpoetry.com/MyriadMusings

[Jozef Neumann]

Planes and buzzards

the plane barely moves,
almost stands still in the
vague air. it loses swaths
of kerosene in fine lines
that dissolve instantly.
four more planes lined
up behind in a string of
lights stretched along
the air corridor over the
motorway.

he turns off the radio and
counts the seconds, as
usual. at 20, the first one is
right in front of his windshield,
displacing the sky. he can
almost touch its belly, before
it disappears over the car
top with a husky roar, like
a giant metal reptile.

he turns the radio back on.
never an accident in all
these years, he thinks, as
his eye catches the dead
buzzard at the side of the

road. it has been lying there
for days. one wing is up
with the feathers fanned
out. it moves slightly as
he drives past.

Jozef Neumann is living in Wiesbaden, Germany. He writes
poems and short stories when he is not making music.
Allpoetry.com/Jozef_Neumann

[Alwyn Barddylbach]

Dreamcatcher

Boy standing under
moonlit lamp post
in the street;

sky buddha said

Three times the
lamp post drops
sentinel on his head

Moon landing
swooning nocturne
maybe dead

Verdant dreams
heaven's willow
bleeds upon my bed.

City bus lies idle
on a street
no driver

Take me
somewhere special
for a fiver

Come dive
with me into the
endless river

Call me crazy
lady over
my blue fever.

I am mobile
all forever
angel white;

sky buddha said

God's web is
high and mighty
as a kite

Save his sacred
pillow in the cloud
out of sight

Boy sleeps
sweetly sobbing
all is right.

Dreams catch fire
light and thunder
angry sprite

Moonbeams
bloom grazing
on the ocean bight

Whales wade
in starlight stealth
on their maiden flight

Boy below
the street lamp
fingers razor bright.

Roaring wings
of time caught
in newborn fog

Orange tiger
hunts the
midnight dog

Neptune's eyes
blaze in the
morning rise

Gaze through
sunny eyelids
intrepid old and wise.

Earth is rising
surging on its
crescent edge

Mesmerising
sun baked soils
and canyon sedge

Beneath the giant
banyan tree sickle
gleaming

Boy stands
with sack of stolen
secrets dreaming;

sky buddha said

Heart still beating
time to catch this
orphan's breath.

_____

Somewhere in the dreamtime between surrealism and minimalism
is a poem called Aussie Haiku - AB Blue Mountains.
Allpoetry.com/Barddylbach

[Mary C. Galindo]

The Claim of Heritage

An immigrant farmer with his family
working the fields on the Dakota prairie.
With seven young daughters, he eyed
the neighbors' sons for prospective husbands.

These four sisters not wanting that
took off to homesteading, each one
their own plot, proving up a claim,
receiving title from President Wilson.

Each one built their own sod house-
lots cornered together - gardens planted ,
horse riding was a must as was the hunting,
using a rifle became a necessity
come Saturday picnics and parties in town

lively stories of their lives homesteading told
through the years of the best time of their lives.
Some lived long lives even to their nineties. After
this adventure they became teachers and seamstresses.

My grandmother was not one of these
courageous sisters and later on
was a suffragette fighting for
freedom, the right to vote. A new
and noble cause. We all win.

Years on and finally with husbands,
children and then grandchildren,
these sisters left a grand heritage of
teachers, lawyers, soldiers, doctors,
farmers and even a city mayor.

It is a story to be proud of as a descendant.
How can I ever live up to such courage
In giving back some of this merit.
The past in our lives defines our
claim. This is my claim to a noble heritage.

Mary (grandmakay) is from N.D, lived in Guatemala, El Salvador, Venezuela. Currently living in Utah. She has always loved writing and poetry is a favored expression. Writing calms a reflective spirit. Allpoetry.com/grandmakay39

[Jozef Neumann]

motorcycles

narrow streets along hillsides
greens and greys shine and fade
under sun and heavy rain on
an isle of men among them Joey
on his knees long wild hair
over his face colored icons on
his leather jacket cigarette in
his mouth working motors and
frames with greasy fingers
sleeping in his truck between
races his dirt diamond shining
so bright it blinds the eye

Jozef Neumann is living in Wiesbaden, Germany. He writes
poems and short stories when he is not making music.
Allpoetry.com/Jozef_Neumann

[Nancy May]

Start Continent

Spain tale
dress November dew;
cleave quill delight!
coast night -
acrobat nook dice.

Spain tale!
eye flounce newt -
flute jolt rain,
dress Spain!
fiddle rift plank -

abacus dare
fickle toss pear.
rest spice.
fleck dime treat -
Spain tale!

Susan N Aassahde is an experimental and micro poet. She is a contributor to Eskimo Pie, Down in the Dirt, Poetry Pea and Plum Tree Tavern. Allpoetry.com/Susan_N_Aassahde

[Lorri Ventura]

A Bostonian

His home is a rag-filled refrigerator box
Propped crookedly on broken sidewalk
Alongside the Boston Common

When I ask him his name
He says, "Just call me 'Least of Your Brothers,'
Then winks conspiratorially

He tugs off mismatched gloves
To jab his raw fingers
Into his tepid cup of Dunkin'
Before gulping its dregs

Coffee trickles through his beard
As he offers a sip from the empty cup
To a passerby
Who squawks in protest
Before bolting to the other side of Tremont Street

The gold-gilded State House dome
Shines down on him
As his gnarled fingers weave gently
Through the yarn hair of a grimy, one-eyed, Raggedy Ann
Propped in his lap

Every so often
He leans forward and kisses the top of the doll's head
With a sweetness that brings tears to my eyes

Seeing people turn their faces away
As they rush past
Pretending not to see him
He waves and grins lopsidedly
Showing three wobbly teeth and chortling,
"Smile! I won't hurt you! Have a nice day!"

I squint through the sunlight
As I watch him from the nearest corner
I think I see
A halo encircling his head.

––––––––––––––––

Lorri Ventura is a retired special education administrator living in Massachusetts. She is new to poetry-writing; her works have been featured in Songs to the Sun and in Poetry Is a Mountain. Allpoetry.com/Lorri_Ventura

[Douglas Pinchen]

The Pith Helmet

Incredibly - I have to say,
My pith helmet is on the way,
The 'Khaki Cove' they say I am,
Who's rather like a chameleon.

The baggage packed and stored aboard,
All ready here to take abroad,
The survey sticks and canvas tents,
Acutely measured for Godly bent.

The native-hard colonial crew,
Have caused a stirring and to-do,
For in their quarters we discover,
Chinese tea for one another!

And what's more our navigator,
Arrived from Dublin, - although much later
The crow's nest was of course quite tested,
The bird's fair-weathered now and nested.

The Captain's plank - a diving board,
In case the sailors got too bored,
And down there in the kitchen grand,
Lobsters offered - like contraband.

The sails were set of Indian cloth,
To bare the Doldrums and the moth,
And so: forsooth! Southampton Water!
The laden ship - your mind - it caught yer!

The boat - it's name - I cannot tell,
It trapped me in its foggy spell,
It's in amongst what I remember:
Topography put out to tender.

Rugged terrain, wildest coast,
Tropicana at it's most,
Friendly and unfriendly peoples,
Trade and toil with rusty cash tills.

A farmer prodding at his cattle,
The miller's work - a daily battle,
Policemen marching up the street,
Ministers daring noon day heat!

All this and more is what we found,
As we dug for holy ground,
And artifacts and missing links,
Compounded into whom who thinks.

Doug Pinchen is from Bulawayo, Africa. Incarcerated for mental health difficulties, it opened new ideas about ironic surrealism in life and the social Geography he experienced there and in England. Allpoetry.com/Doug_Pinchen

[Gavin Brosche]

A Hard Town for Poets

I.

Damn
this is a hard town for poets

So far journeyed
seed and blood upon this
ever caressed asphalt
machine wrapped
million year fueled

My Goddess
wipe clean this rationality
with the shining white cloth
of my infinite madness

Many times have I sat
watching that fragile setting fire
gaudy paint sky and sea
fairy like
your dream city lights
have stealthy crept upon the rising dusk

They never witnessed
those wordy smiths of old
this glistening mandala

of a brood magnificent and deadly
flung upon this Earth

To those crafty tellers
and to you
fruit of the galactic diaspora to be
I offer these scribbles and challenge you
to send me same
spiral spinning
fire gassy cloud fringes of star birth

Hear me, not read, heard
speak aloud this subjective symbolic
representation of reality
caress it tongue and lip
like a one sugared coffee tang
after a dark crazy horse night

So many words
flung into an empty eve
an angel of sacrifice my only audience
spat like our beautiful technology
home to our millennial offspring
brave weeds

All day I write
for the curse and blessing is upon me
I cannot aught else do
for all else is naught

Ah, Vladimir Mayakovsky
my Milton Christ
game three of your roulette
wrought hope and tears more than any
black and red wheel of travesty
spun in this high roller's room

We are not hollow men
we never were
always flesh blood and bone
star seeded optimism
pressed into a cavernous echoing world

The noble sung braves of Troy
Aenid's heroes
or that infernal crew
cast into sulfured boiling lake are but
wordy practice for these times
where the least of us walks
morning drowsy, shower fresh
warriors of times that never
ever will be again
lest some far flung world
births, messy and ravenous
a city child upon
another piteous globe

What does ring hollow
reverberates maddeningly
is this clanging money fuck

bred of Verona's bashing boys
'a means for the distribution of resources'

No, I will not stop
into the ten year besieged city of lit
will I cunning send this
wooden horse of words
out now my siblings
while drunk they sleep
open wide the gates
send in the night fleet
dogs of peace
slipped fearlessly
and burn down these temples of commerce

To the market!
To the market hence!

II.

A bag of Tunney's dark shag
like him of that fantasy real
on Baker Street sat piping
a puzzling case
I roll and smoke
lipping dark Java's brew
contemplating my market wend

Eden's bounty tabled high
colour, taste, scent, texture

dancing through that humble murmur
of Earth's collected fruit
care not for medium of exchange
this was and always will be

That gentle walk
any haughty thoughts has repelled
and only more challenge
to my muse has thrown

Even the most lonely refugee
of a nights bawd
who, penless, sits watching as I
mocks my describing

How so more
children billions
vessels of hope
grails of endless evolution
loving, breeding, flinging themselves
through the cold black ballroom of space
dancing complex back and forth
gesture and bow to the shimmering music
of massy spheres lyre
time blown

———————————

And I set my heart to know wisdom and to know madness and
folly. I perceived that this also is grasping for the wind.' -
Ecclesiastes. Allpoetry.com/GovindaX

[Mary Scattergood]

Granny's Brown House

My grandmother's house in Philadelphia,
every inch brown wood,
I sat in a mahogany chair,
enduring the old wood table, spill of good wine marked with
the voices of the past;
those days when their prayers spoke.

On the wall a mottled mirror
I saw no shadow of myself,
but the resemblance of ancestors
sprinkled chips of brown moles on their skin,
primping before their portraits, their shadows
leaned in,
history on my back,

Am a creative older person, who has never seriously attempted
writing poetry until very recently. I am a former teacher and artist.
A chronic illness led me to try my hand at poetry.
Allpoetry.com/Poetgreen53

[Beverley Wilcock]

Renewal

Alone and broken
but determined
and resolute
this life will not bury her

anchored in fresh courage
this pain must compensate
so it comes to a head
it's time to start a new life

thus the past must pay
to prevent a recurrence
and looking up
she has nothing left to lose

Vernietiging (translated above)

In gedagte verlore
besig om te vergaan
en te wonder
wat is die nut van bestaan

niks maak sin
soos angs omring

en onsekerheid oorwin
wat is tog oor om te gun

g'n rus of stilte
net opdraande
en bulte
dis die vernaamste

al smeek sy
soebat haar knieë blou
daar's geen vrede te kry
sy bly afgeknou
wind geteister
weggeroes
verbyster
verwoes

I am a devoted language practitioner and poet. I teach and enjoy as many languages as I am able and use written words to express what I cannot in any other way. Allpoetry.com/BW....

[David I Mayerhoff]

In A Foreign Land

Off the cruise ship we were sailing
down the plank,
a group of us for the day on the island
I hike towards the outdoor sale
she veers by way of eateries
he samples the island rums

Bargaining with store owners
rummaging through clothes
we meet up at the fishing village
the smell of sea and scales
with rounds of tequila on our woozy brains

Now brimming with hats
lotion at the ready
she laughs hysterically
at our reflections
egging us deeper into the land
I dance to rhythms not played
while he plays the music not heard

Gills of ugly are sold from the barrels
to eat
maybe to drink with
and throw up after

All a distant memory back onboard
as the sun sets
and we sail towards the moon
and our cabins to sleep it off
a smile etched on our faces and scrapbooks

David I Mayerhoff is an emerging literary writer, an established scientific author, and a Clinical Professor of Psychiatry. Allpoetry.com/David_Mayerhoff

[Arlice W. Davenport]

The Light of Love

Diffused rays of lengthening light
scoot across the hardwood floor
and pool on the space where we last lay together.

A long yellow-pine slat of wood
gleams in the afternoon sun.
A bump of lacquer breaks the surface.

For eons, we have coaxed each other
into the light, bearing down upon us
in ever-whitening stripes of purification.

Our love *is* the light, seeping through
the dark crevices of our hearts,
scouring the deep recesses of shadow and doubt.

The floor creaks as we glide across it,
hardy survivor of this hundred-year-old house.
Our love creaks as the past thrusts itself into the present.

We cannot grasp it, but we feel its warmth
wash over us again and again. We know
the radiance of love overcomes all oblivion.

Love and light go together like hardwood floors and lacquer. Love
lights all our inner darkness, makes us free to be creative and
empathetic. This poem tries to capture that dynamic of love and
light. Allpoetry.com/arliced

[Jenny Middleton]

Forget-Me-Nots

Skimming the lake and thrown in fun, a stone
bounced before us, a flint, grey and hewn
from cliffs chipped by centuries and strewn
with veined whorls resembling a heart grown

and patterned with beating veins of all known
time. You saved it and then sent it travelling
to me through red letter boxes to my home.
This new journey fresh with your affirming

hands and its presence, burnt with eddying,
kinetic dance to wake my still thoughts' sleep
and sew them firmly to your own, mingling
touch and taste and breath then together leap

beyond ourselves and bind as soft garlands
of forget-me-nots do joining our hands.

Jenny Middleton lives and works in London. She is a working
mum and loves walking, gardening and her very crazy cats.
Allpoetry.com/Jenny_Middleton

[Robert Buck]

The Iron Gate

A shallow day is always late

Crystal Jones staggers her withdrawal from the nigh side of suicide
she strays and struts the johns of Broker-hill, dangerous green
light district where hustlers are buttoned-down and tied.

Urban reptiles tricking their fate

Betwixt the buy-poles of sex and power a steepled stump crosses
this hollow neck of sin and saves the city of the plain from
brimstone rain, a moral badge redeeming the redeemers of
pleasure and of pain.

A collared lizard smokes in wait

Poor-mans' Catholic preys on fortunes' tithing wakes, takes
nipping breaks and rakes the golden gutter for the beauty biter,
side-wound viper rattling cornered wolves howling the rescued
wrecks for their own rock-candied sakes.

The meeting at the Iron Gate

Brown-eyed piper promises he'll deliver with a sucking line by all
that's fine - give up the wasting ghost for tasting of the heavenly
host. Blue-eyed sniper fixes the sanctimonious sayer with a purr
and smiles another boast.

Who is the date?

Snake of the street stares down his slur. Disguised defender smells her spur. Then there occurs a Holy Stir.

The Iron Gate............... closes............ slowly............ between.

She walks by way the gaudy atrium, opens the door of commons, prays her sign and hallows the wine.

He stalks away the mausoleum, defiles the shaman's symbol, swears his sign and lies with the swine.

Repulsive lodestone laws dictate and philosophy riddles where we concentrate -

Beware you become, what you hate.

I am retired from counseling and needing some. I have been writing poetry for about thirty years. I am a one-percenter that you may have heard about; one out of a hundred of my poems is any good. Allpoetry.com/bobbing

[Marilyn Griffin]

Surfing with sharks

In the slash of
lash-whipped eyes,
the darting mass
of fin sails-
their wind gales
sear the sea

a cut above

vapid glances from
this sanctified sea people
tingle toes and
tangle seaweed
knotting grasses and
ankle leashes
in fast releases

board burping the
choppy air and
sloppy angles of
body dropping

eliding panic
gliding spooked
and clucked

reaping waves in
whole sets of salvation

I ride above them
with my legs attached

_____

I really love AP, a chance to write about my collection of
memories that burble to the surface. Thanks Kevin for this
wonderful place! Allpoetry.com/Greeningofautumn

[Juan Pablo Segovia]

Do not cry for me

Don't be sad the day I die
my presence and my absence
they are only temporary.

Bring me roses, I love roses,
beautiful but little they last,
they also die once cut

Dreams that disappear,
anxieties that no longer exist,
loves that we leave behind,
loves that we follow.

As I am buried
I want to hear the laughter
of children playing

Do not cry for me,
don't cry for me or for my absence.
Cry because I am going home.

No llores por mi (Translated from)

No te entristezcas el dia que muera
mi presencia y mi ausencia
son solo temporarias.

Tráeme rosas, amo las rosas
bellas pero poco duran,
tambien mueren una vez cortadas

Sueños que desaparecen,
angustias que ya no existen,
amores que dejo o que seguiré

Segun me entierren
quiero oir la risa de niños jugando

No llores porque estoy muerto,
no llores por mi o por mi ausencia,
llora porque regreso a Dios

———————————

Retired, live in U S, California. Emigrated from Cuba
I like to write poetry as past time and also gardening.
Have a beautiful grandson that also lives in California. Very
smart, like his mother Allpoetry.com/Juan_Pablo_Segov

[Carl Wayne Jent]

Harvest

Rapture was so gentle, taping the door
fresh feet scampering, across the kitchen floor
broken eggs sizzling, breakfast in the air
timely was served, all wanted to share

Corps of men arrived at harvest field
rippled though crops, checking on the yield
heat wave ended, with the cool autumn rain
body over worked, legs have been strained

Crest of moon means daily work ends
taste of harvest, dinner meal preparation begins
torn shirts, muddy shoes, dine wearing smiles
void of complaints, after all the miles

Smell of love, covered our nightly feast
crimson skies glow fading, back toward east
roots established, over a hundred years ago
mold and cold in month to show

Song sung quietly, soon time for bed
fight for life, the bible is read
mindless men now resting in their sleep
touch from God, lets their spirit keep

The poems I write, I write for comfort. I have wrote several, I read
and ponder life's journey and feel a little better about my
existence. I believe life is wonderful and Earth a place to behold.
Allpoetry.com/Waynejent

88

[Joseph Phillip De Marco]

The Most Sacred Voyage

they humbly came with soft handmade bundles from across the
vast ocean
infants wrapped in meek heirloom cloth facing often dark
clouded sky and choppy restless sea
snug from the cold against momma's warm near raw breasts yet
often still enough to calm the worried men
into humming cherished familiar lullabies and into fond tender
memories biting softly on worn pipe stems and anxious
hoping to see feel and touch liberty a simple ecstasy come real

indelicate faded scarved and heavily garbed women and sternly
capped rugged calloused handed men bathing carefully with olive
oil purifying the voyage with its blessings and courtesy
all hearts guiding safe yet uncertain passage; sacred souls yearning
to plant roots secured
in crafted sheaths planning vineyards for hosts and new found
friends with skilled hands
and honor and gift a new land made of wood turning cities into
beautiful emerging carved casts and smooth cement foundations
and lay brick with stone monuments as solemn gratitude;
bold and generous offerings from sacrifice and sweat; selfless and
determined to please family heaven and AMERICA all craving for
them to arrive

I observe and write with fury and twisted humor. I have been
writing verse since I was 12, now I'm a substitute teacher and
tutor. I earned a B.A. in English Literature and an A.A.S. in
Criminal Justice. Allpoetry.com/Joedemarco171

[Krishna V Ramavat]

Spring on Sand

On a walk through the valley during this brilliant season
I'm awed by His painting, its beauty beyond reason

Chromatic paths paved by Plum and Palo verde Yellow
Some Yucca here, Oleander there and dabs of Desert Willow

I see the Roses gaily bloom among the shady pine
And breathe the bliss of Star-Jasmine passing by its vine

Soaking the briefly gentle Sun, lawns spread south and east
As Rosemary entices bees to her rather memorable feast

Rubbing their marble eyes and casting wariness aside
Bunnies browse the roads seeking an adventurous ride

And for the annual finale Knight Cactus' guard is keen
As amongst the thorn emerges his precious flowery queen

Empty threats of dull cloud brought in by moody wind
Mocks trees and bullies bugs keeping with desert trend

And yet Spring flourishes amply on these arid lands
Life and beauty caper along these resilient sands!

Krishna is from Henderson, Nevada. Poetry is her favorite form for expressing the deepest emotions in life. Allpoetry.com/Kris-unbound

[Kenny Reeves]

I remember

I remember her eyes
the most

dark holes that would
eat their young
framed in aging skin
wrung out by the wrath
of an angry sun

she would sit for hours
shrinking cigarettes to nubs
thrumming the air with her
mindless muddle

her fingers crowned
obscenely scarlet
playing the rudiments of
a distant drum

she wore her mother's fears
like a prized tiara
and lingered at the window

waiting for a carriage
that would never come

yes

I remember those eyes
the most

and how she hated life
so perfectly

I wish I could say that this poem was fictional or vicarious. It is
neither. This is where I grew up. Allpoetry.com/Wayward_Son

[David I Mayerhoff]

The Unforgotten Night

Went to bed all tucked in
not a peep in the dark
the sleep would be a win

Dreams were many
I was cooking a stew
washing it down
with a nice cold brew

Painted the kitchen
color off red
thought of doing the basement
but better off when dead

Rug needed sweeping
and vacuum I did
had a little desert
dripping all over the bib

Opened the front door
to check out the street
boy was it cold
and bereft of any heat

Checked out the telly
to see what was playing

fidgeted with the remote
until I was fading

Back to bed
nothing really lost
since I knew this was a dream
lived at any cost

Until the next morning when I awoke
all foggy and spent
and opened my eyes
to a house that I rent

Decked out in shambles
with my hand bandaged in gauze
when it hit me like bricks -
I was the cause

———————————

David I Mayerhoff is an emerging writer, an established scientific
author and a Clinical Professor of Psychiatry. He grew up on
Long Island and resides in New Jersey.
Allpoetry.com/David_Mayerhoff

[Joseph Phillip De Marco]

The Zoo

anti frost papers had no noise
an army of noisy attitudes
behind bare barred zoo of baboons
amphibians creep into crevices before night
mint of silver disappears into liquid feed
frenzy escapes no one before light
the apes bewildered amazed and join
the scope narrow and thin persuade
the taverns cry in vain in sober relief
the milk is safe the babies' guard
the ladies of the night prepare for more
dogs are ready to provide the sum
jugglers evade the landlord's sweep
no tender is earned enough to keep at bay
the copper, the court, the cell nor hell at one's feet

I observe and write with fury and twisted humor. I have been writing verse since I was 12, now I'm a substitute teacher and tutor. I earned a B.A. in English Literature and an A.A.S. in Criminal Justice. Allpoetry.com/Joedemarco171

[Ashantae L Stone]

Autumn

Crisp orange and yellow ribbon leaves
fall with the breeze of golden trees
with the sun being of a delight
I inhale the fragrance of the fresh air
watching the birds fly south
to avoid north's cold snare
Within my cozy hammock
having myself snugged tight
reminiscing about how autumn
is the cause for the romance

Writing short stories and poems has become a safe place for me to share my life lessons and blessings, with the aspiration to help others in any positively way possible. Allpoetry.com/BLove

[Daniel Duna]

Petal Jumpers

Plump little bumblebee, stumbling mid air
like a sot who had one too many plus one.
Bumbles gleefully, busy bee buzzing
from flower to flower, stamen to stamen,
tending his garden of sweet nectar.
This sun-warmed pile of lush fur coated,
sticky and yellow ochre-powdered gold
spewing forth by satiated pod like anthers.
His abdomen flicking against the stigma,
like the nervous tick of an old pantomime,
unintentional, he fertilizes it effortlessly
while adhering to daily scheduled harvesting,
as a busy bumblebee's chores are never done.

I am a 55 year old who loves to dabble in writing my thoughts and experiences on paper. My hobbies include guitar, songwriting/recording, art work, and scale model building. Allpoetry.com/buddho

[Rueneta Barclay]

In The 1800s

It was in the late 1800s
In that small quiet Texas town
Two oil lamps & a candle
Lit the home all dark & brown.

In the distance hooves were coming and
Range riders pushing ground
Searching for the Doc's good work,
Who would save this man, shot down.

The night was dark and lonely
And stillness filled the air,
No oil lamp in this room that night
Could burn light bright enough.

Hurriedly, floor plugs were set,
The size too small for guns,
Only food, & remedies would pass to injuries on the ground.

Jesse James & men could rest a bit, but then they had to go.
The morning sun would be on time, & they didn't want a show...

The water in the well was all the horses had to have
For when the morrow day would break,
They'd be out of town, Hico!

I am Rueneta Barclay & a Texas resident for almost half a century. I began writing poetry in 1997, and I find it comes in spurts. I enjoy other's accomplishments, & like encouraging them to write. Allpoetry.com/Rueneta_Barclay

[Madeleine McLaughlin]

The Snowball Fight

At five o'clock
we waited for Dad in the falling snow
it lay up to our knees around us all
minutes passed - Dad drove up

He opened his car door, bent down
and made a snowball
he threw it at us and we laughed
and tossed one back

Mom joined in, something she never did
Dad, Mom, my brother and sister threw and threw
and laughed and laughed
we ended up down in the ravine at the end of the street

The laughter, the light snow falling
the glint of white in the dark

_____

Madeleine McLaughlin is a writer of fiction as well as poetry. She has digitally published award winning e-books. She lives in Ottawa, Ontario. Allpoetry.com/celadia

[Michael Fuller]

Grand dad's box

Cleaning out the old closet
Removing old shoes and clothes
A box stuck at the back
An attractive, interesting old box
Opening with bated breath
Ancestors fly out circling my head
Grand dad's old watch
Time stands still
An ornate silver hairbrush
A brush that's stroked a million hairs
Generations of ladies flood out
Old folded newspapers
Stories of battles and wars past
Tales and talk of bravery and honour
The birth of a nation
Notebooks and a diary
Spreading the ghosts of the past
All in grand dad's box
Found in the back of the old closet

I love my part of Australia, it is full of colour which fuels my
writing, my black soil at home on the mighty Macquarie River.
I started writing to cope with the grief of losing my friend to
cancer. Allpoetry.com/Michael_Fuller67

[David I Mayerhoff]

A Perfect Evening

Lights lay dim cabaret style
with the song of jazz
swooning in my ears
starving to hear more
than just music

eyes lock eyes
in the embrace of legend
as my scotch
numbs my brakes
and eggs me on

you are bathed in shadow
wearing a growl like a leopard skin
beckoning the wild to stalk the night

the air convulses in the chemistry between us
like a buyer at an auction,
the wine bids you on
with the hour clock injecting a look
of stop this now

the silence speaks volumes
to fill the books of a shelf
we don't whisper
lest a vacuum

uproot the quiet

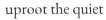

David I Mayerhoff is an emerging writer, an established scientific
author and a Clinical Professor of Psychiatry. He grew up on
Long Island and now resides in New Jersey.
Allpoetry.com/David_Mayerhoff

[Kylie Jensen]

One red shoe

I watched through
smudged handprints
from our school bus window

one red shoe
sits solely on fresh
skid marks that
line the highway
only seconds before
there were two shoes
that contained a pair of
running feet

in an orange sedan
its windscreen shattered
sits a man, his face
palest white
staring bleakly to the wayside
watching as a child's mother
runs toward a broken body

and that harrowing scream
that escapes her mouth
has never left my ears...

Kylie Jensen is from Townsville, QLD, Australia. She's has been writing since she was 15, and is now 45. When not writing you can find her swimming at the beach or enjoying her gorgeous grandchildren. Allpoetry.com/Kylie_Jensen

[Joshua Appleby]

finding

three years I spent
tattooed to the east--
a moving stain
but I swear I could hear my name
in the pulse

I rode the greyhound
in the blackness of night
so I didn't have to see
what was left behind

in the morning
I watched the movement of strangers
and did not write poetry
because they spoke it in their hellos
their goodbyes
the way they walked past each other
and didn't flinch,
didn't run

I trekked mud
all throughout their pretty streets
but the cleaning man still sung
behind me
still smiled
said I will come back one day

return like rain
and pray for forgiveness
on my clean knees

and you cannot see the winds of change
you can only breathe it in

on the shore I heard it call for me
like an old song
like an unfinished poem

so I left my footprints
on the east
like wet graffiti

and all night
near mama's bedside
I could feel
the salt air
the white foam
dragging my monuments
into the tide

_____

I'm from Georgia and I fell in love with the creativity and freedom
of expression found in free verse and slam/spoken word poetry.
Allpoetry.com/blue_lion

[Tobias Bang Søgaard]

White Lilies

I kneel by lilies white against black stone
the clouds are grey but sun is shining bright
me by myself, a garden full of bones
I kneel by lilies white against black stone
forgiveness wins, departure is postponed
"Do not go gentle into that good night"
The quote weighs heavier against black stone
yet clouds have fled, and sun is shining bright

———————————

I am an Aarhus-based amateur writer, and I study linguistics. I find my inspiration from nature or my own struggles. Writing helps me cope. I can cook minute rice in only 58 seconds. Allpoetry.com/Tobi-Wan_Kenobi

[Kayla Nakabasa]

Bhutan's Majesty

Your gaze is magnificent.
Your smiling face is like a lotus
immersed in the sun,

like gazelles on the plains
dancing without fear,
prancing in the joy of life.

Your eyes are endless pools
filled with clusters of stars
bathing the sky on cloudless nights.

This poem is for the current king of Druk Yul, whom is a
beautiful person, inside and out. I've been enamored by him for
about 15 years now and the love just keeps growing.
Allpoetry.com/Broken_Zipper

[Richard Fairchild]

Spanish Sun-glow

Sunset blues! The Orange hues
the Sun rides, regal,
Low in the Sky,
Sinking slowly
As our spirits call time
on another Sultry, sleepy Spanish
Day.

The crimson tide mirrors
the diurnal-nocturnal
ebb and flow
Of our very existence
The essence of our
Ethereal, fleeting moments
Of bright unbridled joy,
Grains of golden sand: Constantly washed away
By the turquoise waters,
Aquamarine,
Lapping at our feet of clinging clay: mud-grey.

At last, the Moon-rise,
Melancholic: the purpling sky,
A brilliant backdrop canvas
To a million and one orange-white
Drizzled paint splattered stars,
Shining bright

Different ambience in this warm velvet night.
Waiting on a new bright orange dawn.

All at once, the sky lightens,
Gradual gradations of colour,
The holy artist,
Who designed the rainbow,
Roy G Biv,
Stars put to flight,
As drained through a giant cosmic sieve!

Sunrise red! Orange saltpeter
Explosions in the sky.
The early-morn fishermen
Take their primitive coral boats
Out to sea:
To catch fish of many hues,
Whites, crimsons, pinks, brilliant blues! Sand-Speckled fins.
And another red-hot Mediterranean day begins.

———————————

Rich F is from Bristol, England. I am a university academic - in addition to writing poetry, I play blues guitar, and find both activities very emotional. Allpoetry.com/Rich_F

[Janet Paulin]

Spider in my Shower

A spider decided to reside in my shower.
It looks peaceful, peeking through the steam;
Reminds me of snow macaques native to Japan on Natgeo,
simmering in rock spas, perpetually placid
except, I see slim legs tipped with a sharp travesty of toes,
too hard to count with soap sodden eyes.
Like goblet drums in Egypt announcing my heartbeat,
I snap out of a day dream, I'm prone to those;
I'm troubled by this thought -- that micro,
seemingly trivial decisions are the truest test of character.
At what other juncture do we get to play Jehovah,
with only ourselves and the weaker other as witness?
The glass door whines as it swings open, slower than usual,
skipping the ritual of squeegeeing the surface.
I call husband in flirty feigned fright,
incriminating the sinister squatter in the shower.
He picks it up with diplomatic grace,
greeting in a language assuaged by those who don't fear spiders.
Bringing it to a spot near the Bromeliad's cup,
his finger serves as bridge between the critter's friend
and its new home.

I'm a restless old soul drawn to the shores that sparkle under the Southern sun. Like a moth dancing around an oil lamp, my life is a constant struggle between playing with fire and getting burnt. Allpoetry.com/Onyx

[Kimberly McNeil]

Birth

Newborns escape the womb
as monstrous human forces
triangulate and funnel
the smoothly muscled uterus
with the squeezing force
of a wrestling half Nelson.
Screaming, crying, slippery, shiny
like a greased watermelon
warm and wiggling between my hands.
I almost dropped a few,
ruled no fumble on review.
A momentary panic
called birth.

Kimberly McNeil, MD is a poet and artist who has retired and lives spontaneously in Florida. Her only child, Dashiell, died November 2018 in a motor vehicle accident.
Allpoetry.com/Dashpatı

116

[Hannah Lipman]

Gratitude

From room to room I see
the tree branch shadow dance,
The outside world,
quilting quiet movement
on my living room walls,

And I sit by the window,
in awe of the tallness waving around me.
Sunshine resting in the hammocks of my lashes,
Stillness moves my thoughts to rest.

This is what safety tastes like,
Whisper breath, gliding like a slow wave kissing shore, and
back out to source for more.

Life is good when in my home,
alone,
with my thoughts and
breath.

It wasn't always like this.

_____

Hannah Lipman has been exhaling thoughts on paper since her
teen years. She lives in CT up on a hill.
Allpoetry.com/Poetunderglass

[Ashwini Kumar Rath]
Saint of Woolsthorpe

An old walled garden,
teeming with mortals -
men and women, peeping
into a whole new world
with the mind's eye
that is big and bold.

Apples honour gravity,
yet the mind, the world -
calculus, optics,
laws of motion,
theoretical physics born.

Muddy pavements
with dark sheds,
in rural luxury
of the manor house,
World seems different
for Sir Isaac Newton -
The Saint of Woolsthorpe.

_____

Ashwini learnt physics and later became an entrepreneur in digital
technologies. Well-travelled, he writes and speaks on various
topics. He loves Nature and rural life. Allpoetry.com/Akrath

[Gilda Math]

African Landscape Musings

In my dreams I would like
to climb up to the summit,
of that high African mountain
and breathe in the clean air,
behold the orange sunrise
awakening the slumbering land!

With its misty warm glow
the stream of inspiration flows
feeling the spirit ascending
in the midst of the awakening
pristine new morning and far
from the boisterous crowd!

———————————

I live in Florida with my husband and pet birds. One of my interests, besides poetry is to travel abroad, fueled by my love of foreign languages and cultures. Allpoetry.com/Gilda_Castillo

[Carolyn Caudle Castle]

Adventure With Pokey

Pokey wants an adventure today.
Let's tag along and watch her at play.
Her shell is safe as a home so warm,
It calms her from a coming storm..

Like 'pop goes the weasel' she popped out her head
Next comes four legs like four pegs on which she sped.
Hearing the brush as we stepped in the twigs, she saw red.
Slowing our approach, she stays out instead.

Carolyn is from the big state of Texas. My reason for living is
Jesus, God's only Son, everyone's Saviour after death for eternity,
if accepted so here... thus most of my poetry relates to Him.
Allpoetry.com/CarolynCaudleCas

[Dylan Clark]

The breeze

The sweet embrace of the autumnal wind on your face,
Brisk, refreshing.
The smell of the last lawn clippings,
The rustle of leaves tumbling down the sidewalk
Football on the family TV
Warm apple cider in your belly
Turtle necks changing to turtle doves
A childhood of jumping into leaves
All these things from the embrace
Of another autumnal breeze

_____

From Madison WI, poetry is how I unwind for the day, and ease my stress away. Aside from working in kitchens as a full time cook, I've been prompted by those I love to finally share my work with other people. Allpoetry.com/Coachdylan3295

[Ian Lee]

Consternation and Constellations: a rhyme royal

A final walk on that crackling oak floor,
We clutch our hands as lovers one last time,
To the threshold past that bucolic door,
I'll never forget scents from your neck line,
Your dainty perfume of jasmine and lime,
Simultaneously saying goodbye,
Sorrowed constriction as such I could die,

After the rift, I spent the years adrift,
Kisses on that sultry forehead I miss,
Different jobs of nights and morning shifts,
Looking for crumbs, at times I reminisce,
Even crave her ravings and lividness,
Hobo I am, often a farmhand for little,
My look is half-tan, sun-dried and brittle,

An effort to sleep with consternation,
Laying on damp ground by a fading fire,
An empty stare at the constellations,
A 'bull' enforcer leaps from the briar,
"I'll club that head to help you get higher."
No warmth of the sun can replace her beam,
She was the prerequisite for my dreams,

———————————

Noblerot28's youth was spent in K.C. His interests of boxing and writing capture him so that at times he fails to cherish the moment with friends and family. Kind regards for those who handle him. Allpoetry.com/Noblerot28

[Jennifer Randall]

Hanka at Ninety-Five

I struggle to the bedroom on my burning feet
And I must feel my way
With useless eyes
Like blind Gloucester.

My daughter brings her painter.
I hear him say 'white walls will highlight
The white of your linen on your big bed
It will fit perfectly without that black walker
And the white and red cane'

She too wants me dead.

Soon she'll have her wish
And so will I.

———————

Jennifer Randall is from Sydney Australia. She likes swimming in
the ocean. Writing poetry helps her get through winter.
Allpoetry.com/Jennifer_Randall

[Florence Elizabeth Samples]

A Winter's Call

The flames are amber
The night is cold
The stars are shining
The moon is gold

The clouds are hazy
The night owl woes
The trees sway slightly
As the whispering wind blows

The grass is moist
A mist is falling
I shudder helplessly
For winter is calling

———————————

Liz Samples from Irving Texas. The only thing I love more than writing poetry is sharing my poetry.
Allpoetry.com/Liz_Johnson_Samp

[Lisa F. Raines]

Rainy morning - Wouldn't you know it

Cars splash through muddy potholes
and overfilled storm drains, while
hydroplaning on oily streets.

I try to avoid murky puddles,
and swift currents along sidewalks.
Always unlucky, I get drenched by both.

AlisRamie is from North Carolina, USA.
Interests include: philosophy, history, international relations,
poetry, art, design, jazz, funk, and some good old soul.
Allpoetry.com/AlisRamie

[Sandra Poindexter]

My first injection administration

I was a junior in nursing school
my patient was due for an
intramuscular injection in her
gluteous maximus

my instructor was there
breathing down my neck
and my patient was
skin and bones

why couldn't I have someone
with a little fat
now I was worried I'd hit bone
trembling I mentally marked

my spot remembering the
upper outer quadrant rule
to avoid the sciatic nerve
I opened the alcohol pad

cleaning off my mark
I'd been practicing on oranges
but they didn't give feedback
I picked up the syringe

palms sweaty praying
lord let this go well
explaining to my patient
what I was about to do

she knowing I'm a student
I imagined a dart board in my mind
then I inhaled and held my breath
counting silently in my head

one~two~three
bam oh my god I had
inserted the needle now think
ok just pull slightly back on

the syringe to ensure it's
not in a blood vessel
whew no blood now
press on the plunger

it seemed that needle
was in her derrière for
five minutes before I pulled it out
it really wasn't

I passed
another skill
checked off
success
I took a breath

I am a mother, grammie, nurse of 41 years and a poetess. My family, my profession, humor and nature often inspire me. Writing poetry is my passion and my happy place!
Allpoetry.com/Poem_5957

[Kiana ModoLowe]

Black or White

Thick, black smoke rises. Curling,
rolling, reaching for the troposphere;
a belch of expended energy.

Robust, white clouds billow with innocence;
vaporized droplets of simpler times.

Thunderheads roar. Race. Rest.
The squall line a velvet carpet directing my way to you.

Paparazzi lightning; the sky erupts. Rumbles,
draws me closer to the echo of the gentle thrum at your center.

The vault of heaven cries in synchronicity.
Of what was. Of what is. Of what is yet to be.

Enveloped in a cloudburst, I find you.
Liquid sunshine on hot concrete.

The cadence of your chest promises nothing but time,
and soon, two rose petal lips will invite mine.

Fill me with the hope that tomorrow will be
anything but grey.

Kiana ModoLowe is from LaSalle, Ontario, Canada. Typically writing in free verse, she relies on a confident voice clashing with thoughts of false bravado. Allpoetry.com/ModoLowe

[Mary Elizabeth Vanorskie]
Some Dim Light to Work By

Gently lifting
her skim-milk-spilled-over-white
Alabaster-stone skin-- an exceptional
integumentary work of art
of both a simultaneously ghastly
and ethereal, pallid, fragile
necro-glam glow in
post-mortem appearance
in the mood lighting
of the Autopsy Room/Basement--
the Coroner Lifts the Veil
Separating the case of
"Undetermined Causation"
from the case closed via the keen application of Science.
Observes a lightly visible bruising
evident. Concludes
This Planet's Unforgivably Brutal
and that this death is suspicious.

———————————

Born Sept. 24th, '87, to Nancy Vanorskie-Byron at Jackson Memorial Hospital in Miami, Florida. Presently, proudly promoting the election of caring Liberal Public Servants in the upcoming US midterms. Allpoetry.com/Mary_Vanorskie

[Christopher A. Patrick]

Autumn's Beauty

Waking up to brisk mornings
Making a fresh pot of coffee
I step outside to see the view
Enchanted trees are all around
Releasing their leaves
With multiple beautiful colors
Amber, brown and even auburn
The sun is burning hot
While the air remains cool
The leaves from the trees
Fall and flow in the wind
Bringing colors on the ground
As well as through the sky
Providing such a lovely view
Seeing such an enchantment
Can make a man wish
For Autumn to never pass.

I am from Neptune, New Jersey, but reside in South Florida.
Poetry helps me relieve stress and helps me express how I truly
felt. I also enjoy listening to music and training in Muay Thai.
Allpoetry.com/Patrick_CA

[Emeli Dion]

One Planet to Call Home

Bees let the flowers bloom,
Yet their population faces doom.
Within the dirt our footprints are set,
But it's our carbon print that is the Earth's biggest threat.

We throw our trash on the ground,
Letting raccoons choke when it is found.
Turtles look to the moon to find their way,
Yet on the road their carcasses lay.

Plastic floats within the waves,
Horses become farmers' slaves.
Beauty is seen throughout nature,
Yet global warming destroys another glacier

The animals are hiding, the forests are disappearing.
Humans ride in cars and now pollution is appearing.
A street cat gasps for clean air.
Human actions are no longer fair.

The rainforests are dying,
More and more people are crying.
We're destroying our Earth,
And soon it won't be able to sustain new birth.

134

Emeli Dion lives in a small town located in New Hampshire. When she isn't studying for school or working, she enjoys writing and playing guitar. Allpoetry.com/Emeli_Dion

[Lisa F. Raines]

Take Me Home

I remember when I was a child,
singing along with Dad
on long road trips home.

We would sing the oldies;
"You Are My Sunshine"
is still my favorite.

Dad loved the song,
"Take Me Home Country Road."
John Denver was so apropos.

We sang it loudly,
and often, as we rode
through the beautiful
Blue Ridge mountains.

Soon, we arrived to drive
the long country roads
to the farm, the grove,
and the small town nearby.

Now, the farm has a
highway running through it.
The house and the
barn are gone; but,

we still travel to that
pleasant little mountain town
where home and family
will surely be found.

_____

AlisRamie is from North Carolina, USA.
Interests include: philosophy, history, international relations,
poetry, art, design, jazz, funk, and some good old soul.
Allpoetry.com/AlisRamie

[Ann Copland]

Lady in a Bar

Empty
inside, still light outside
in southern Central time.
Dressed and polished;
ready for the night.

Kill
An hour in the bar.
For the Hell of it - H - as in Humor.
Fresh college kid behind the rail.
"Absolute martini, very dry, up, with a twist."

Smile
I ordered simple.
Kid looks at his stock.
We chat. he confesses:
"I've never done this before."

Teach
Art and theory of twist.
He presents a jagged, thick
lemon rind floating like an iceberg.
"Let me show you ...."

Finish
The lesson.

Patient guidance.
Success.
"Thank you, ma'm"

The afterglow of
old age sinks in
as I leave, thinking,
'when you talk ....
... be kind.'

_____

Ann Copland lives in Virginia, looking for the good in everyone
and every day. Retired from government work, friends and
movies missed over the last thirty five years are her entertainment.
Allpoetry.com/Ann_Copland

[Kathryn Kass]

The Shaman's Rattle

Bead and bone,

Seed and stone

Shake this feeling loose.

Invocation

Supplication

Miracles produce.

Bead and bone,

Seed and stone

Call the spirits in.

Revelation

Transformation

Grow another skin.

Bead and bone,

Seed and stone

Welcome in the air.

Inhalation

Exhalation

Breathe a simple prayer.

Bead and bone,

Seed and stone

Tend the sacred fire.

Scintillation

Transmutation

Leap onto the pyre.

Bead and bone,

Seed and stone
Hail the pouring rain.
Reclamation
Germination
Bless with life again.
Bead and bone,
Seed and stone
Spin a thread of mirth.
Animation
Sweet sensation
Dance upon the earth!

––––––––––––––––––

My love of meditation, hypnosis, and shamanic journeying is reflected in my work and poetry. I live near the ocean in sunny, southern California, inspired each day by the beauty of nature. Allpoetry.com/Katekass7

[Deborah F. Thomas]

The Immigrant

He creeps along the river
near the shores where the Gulf Stream lies as he slips into this
Country
with aggrieved and anguished eyes

His ragged clothes and mud-clad shoes with a knapsack on his
back
tired lines etched on his face
from the hopefulness, he lacks

A sordid smell of sweat he wears
like a medal of a soldier
and in his weary arms, a child
crying as he holds her

An immigrant, a dirty word,
emblazoned across his chest
searching for a place to land
a place to work and rest

Fleeing from the tyranny
that rips apart his people
who seek a place to safely pray
a house that bears a steeple

Give me your hand, your bleeding heart
and I'll help you cross the river
and cradle you in Liberty's arms
where freedom shall be delivered

Born and raised in Frederick County, Md
Senior citizen and a Part-time Poet; I write poetry because words
matter and it's a great stress reliever.
Allpoetry.com/Deborah_F_Thomas

[Patricia LeDuc]

A Sweet Summer Day

It's the last day of summer
we have to say goodbye
autumn creeps in quietly
takes us by surprise

a new chill in the air
cooler days and cooler nights ahead
as the sun goes to bed early
then dawn breaks though the darkness
to give us light for the day

the crisp cool of autumn comes tomorrow
so celebrate the last day of summer
but then you'll
be wishing summer hadn't gone away

———————————

Poetry is a creative way to clear my mind and put my thoughts
into words. Mother/Grandmother/Happily Retired. I live in
Middletown, Connecticut Allpoetry.com/Patricia_LeDuc

[Katharine L. Sparrow]

For the Love of Bob

I was thirteen.
Whispers of maternal yearnings
ruffled my pony tails,
and bee-sting breasts
made me self-conscious in a tee shirt.

I still climbed trees.
From the branch of an old, gray locust I heard it—
"cheep! cheep!" like a yellow chick.
But it wasn't a chick.

I dropped to the springtime grass, crouched and looked—
a baby quail,
flecked brown and trembling like an autumn leaf.
I took him home, named him Bob—
(I'd read "That Quail Robert", a favorite book)—
a cardboard box, a bed of dry grass, an upturned jar lid for water.

Each morning I'd wake to Bob, "cheep! cheep! cheep!"
I'd get up and drop some seed in his box,
like a mother who rises in pre-dawn's blackness to an infant's
hungry cry.
I took him outside to teeter in the grass, collected him gently,
and back to the box.

I held him. He nestled in my palm, leaning against my fingers.
I felt his fluffy quivering, his watch-tick heartbeat.
His downy, mini-wings would fold, and he'd closed his bright
eyes,
safe and loved.

One day, in mid-summer, I did not wake to his calling.
Late morning sunlight angled across my bed.

There he was, in his box, still and silent, soft wings
plastered wet to his fragile body,
He had fallen into the jar lid
when he died.
He didn't even look like him.

"He must have had a heart defect or something", my mom
soothed,
"and his mother pushed him from the nest.
They sense these things, you know."

All day I cried. All night I missed his rustling.
In the morning I wrapped him in a cotton handkerchief
and buried him at the edge of the woods,
behind my house.

Only a baby quail. Not a mother's child.
But at thirteen,

his loss was like a rock thrown at my heart—
a whisper of maternal love, a pummeling of sorrow.

I have three grown children now.
But, you know—
when I think of Bob today,
I still
cry.

_____

Katharine L. Sparrow lives on Cape Cod in Massachusetts.
Besides writing poetry, she loves her cats and baseball (Go Red
Sox!) Allpoetry.com/Ksparrow

[Samantha Kriese]

Thawing Hearts

I stood in a coffee shop letting my blood thaw
as I searched the scene for a person that could be you.
Feeling like a fool,
embarrassed by inexperience,
I accepted defeat by a window.

But in the winter's dead air,
you appeared
peering through the window at me
with fear and tundra stiffening your bones.
When you finally took the seat across from me,
your mouth must have been frozen too.

After some nervous shifts
and our wind-burnt cheeks turned to blush,
our conversation started to thaw.
The coldest night of the year
was the warmest my heart had thudded in years.

That night we dared our doubts to meet,
I could feel my life changing
like the wavering rhythms flowing through my chest.

S. A. Kriese is the author of One Who Plays with Paper and Pens.
She lives in Eau Claire, WI and is delighted that her daydreaming
and ideas are becoming more than just ink on a page.
Allpoetry.com/S.A.Kriese

[Ina J Evans]

Tiles mock runways

It's busy
being insane
all the time

minds have
tile floors mocking
a runway
toss departed roses'
petals down,
unroll
my red carpet
I'm on my way
to crack my mirror
and, say goodbye, again
my art, is dying
If done exceptionally well
Would I still be here repeating myself?

———————————

From Atlanta GA. Poetry is my art - I paint pictures with words.
I write poems instead of keeping a diary. They are my
confessions. I work as a massage therapist; I also sing and play
piano. Allpoetry.com/Ina_Evans

[Christina Marie Cuevas]
Not looking back

Not looking back
when time changes as the seasons do
we learn to keep moving forward
and not looking back
as a tide runs through the sea of light
like a sailfish (Istiophorus platypterus) flying in the speed of light
most amazing creatures in the ocean
the ocean view is so beautiful
full of all types of fish
small and huge
it's great to see
all types of creatures roam in the that big ocean
like our lives full of things good and bad
but at the end of the day
I'm not looking back no more,
I have so much great things planned in the future
God has me to full fill,
because I don't look back,

Love 69 - Christina Marie Cuevas, a Texas-born writer, graduated from Everest University with a Bachelor Degree of the Paralegal field. Currently, she is working on obtaining a MBA Degree. Allpoetry.com/Love69

[Lisa F. Raines]

Betrayal

I tried so hard to hold it, controlled,
but that single tear rolled silently
down my cheek, belying my true self.

––––––––––––––––––

AlisRamie is from North Carolina, USA.
Interests include: philosophy, history, international relations,
poetry, art, design, jazz, funk, and some good old soul.
Allpoetry.com/AlisRamie

[Paricia LeDuc]

All Is Well For Me Today

The tea kettle is whistling
I hear the toaster go pop
Birds are happily chirping
I wonder what they have to say
it's gonna be a beautiful morning
All is well for me today

In my bathrobe drinking my tea
I put my face to the blue sky
As I watch the world pass by
I see fluffy clouds in the distance
Playing hide and seek with me
All is well for me today

Sirens scream in the distance
Someone is mowing their lawn
A smell so familiar from my memories
Warm winds blow in slowly
Spring is finally upon us again
All is well for me today

———————————

Poetry is a creative way to clear my mind and put my thoughts into words. Mother/Grandmother/Happily retired. I live in Middletown, Connecticut Allpoetry.com/Patricia_LeDuc

[Laura Gallagher]

Mirror Mirror

Mirror mirror on the wall,
Who is this girl I see,
With eyes so big and lips so small,
Is this stranger really me,

Mirror mirror on the wall,
I long to know this face,
With dreams so big and hopes so high,
Better than this place,

Mirror mirror on the wall,
This girl is growing strong,
Her head held high and standing tall,
In this place she does belong,

———————————

Hello, I am Laura, I am from the west of Ireland. Poetry for me is a great way to clarify feelings and put meaning to them. Tones to my poems are journeys we take and overall message of love and light Allpoetry.com/LauraGall

[Gabrielle Antoinette]

"The Poetic Act"

I am just a poet
From another life
Who are you
Why such strife

William Shakespeare said
"All the world's a stage"
I'm just a character player
Acting out life till my 7th age

Paint a pretty picture
In a dainty frame
Legendary colors of a true Picasso
Visionary of the remarkably insane

Gabrielle Antoinette Paris is a Florida Native. Her first poem was published in third grade for a school project. GAbrielle is also an actress and studied with the late Burt Reynolds before he passed
Allpoetry.com/Gabrielle_Paris

[Peter Boadry]

There was a Donkey Named Dave

There was a donkey named Dave

Who found buried gold treasure in a cave

He became the richest donkey in the land

He and his girlfriend would walk hand in hand

On the hot sand

Mave has a mean owner named Clave

It's up to Dave to be brave

He had her to save

By a close shave

So she wouldn't be his slave

All the other donkeys gave a rave

And a wave

And now she was free

To be

With Dave

And she could eat what she craved!

———————————

I've had Few poems published in Anthology's, Boss at Christmas, Mailbox Lady, Mailbox Lady 2, Dear Mom (May 1, 2004), King of Love, and A Heart Beats with One Love, and 1 short story Rescue 911: UFO Allpoetry.com/Frpass

[Stephanie C. Keeley]

Parisa and the Pantry

Parisa wipes her eyes as she looks all around
New to the orphanage, not a smile could be found
Jasmine, peeking over her covers whispers
If you want to play follow me and my sister

The old woman falls asleep about 10
We'll wait a few minutes and then grab Quinn
I promise it's nothing you've ever dreamed
Her eyes are glistening and a smile starts to beam

A little after 10 and the girls have Quinn
Jasmine leads to the pantry and they all go in
Quietly she whispers "please show us the way,
we are all bored and we want to play."

A beautiful land appears from thin air
The darkness is gone, wind is blowing their hair
Giggles and singing can be heard all around
Waterfalls and castles, Parisa's spellbound

Welcome to the Land of the Children Lost
To stay or to visit, a smile it will cost
Play and explore far and wide
There's nothing to fear, no reason to hide

Each castle has different food, snacks, and drinks
You'll see mystical creatures and a fairy that's pink
They all are here because they got lost too
No parents or loved ones, now part of our crew

And if you choose to leave and go back
Simply say out loud "I am done, now backtrack."
Now go off and enjoy your time in this land,
having the time of your lives, without reprimands

Skipping and laughing while clapping their hands,
they head over the hills having a time so grand
The children played all through the night
Choosing not to return and to stay in the light

———————————

I am a wife and mother to three beautiful children. Born and
raised in Indiana, I love spending time with my family and
volunteering. My hobbies include writing, singing, knitting, and
cooking. Allpoetry.com/NightOwl13

[Douglas Pinchen]

The Men from 1894 Tolpuddle

Why are these men here? Some asked,
Their work is well and good,
Are they sending craftsmen now,
To Australia's neighbourhood?
It's said they said:
"The money isn't good enough,
And the hungry do inflict,
'The shilling' has been doctored so the world is in conflict.
Our fathers, sons and brothers slave,
- But long for mindful rest:
Agitation does persist;
And our blood is in the mist!"
How they cried for their fine wives,
And thought of Dorset's shores,
It's a pity the Justice counted them,
Amongst the country's boors.

———————

Doug Pinchen is from Bulawayo, Africa. Incarcerated for mental
health difficulties, it opened new ideas about ironic surrealism in
life and the social Geography he experienced there and in
England. Allpoetry.com/Doug_Pinchen

[Swaytha Sasidharan]

Poetry and Me!

A poet of rules and structures I am not,
Poetry of rhyme, metaphor and simile, not always,
What to me poetry is, a perpetuity to quench,
This unquenchable thirst to write!

Meandering thoughts,
Lassoed by a verse,
A reminiscence, joyous or distressing,
It's not all in the words, but in the reader's perception that
discerns.

What is poetry if not a soothing salve,
Not a goal, but a journey,
Boundaries are constricting,
And poetry, a liberation I find.

———————————

Swaytha Sasidharan is from India and lives in Germany. She loves
all forms of poetry. She is an engineer by profession.
Allpoetry.com/Staardust

[Lisa F. Raines]

Even if It's All of the Time

I want you to have
wonderful memories of us,
even if it's all of the time.

You listen to my poetry,
you look at my art,
even if it's all the time.

You have the patience
of a glacier, but I know
I'm wearing you down.

I'm sorry I do that,
all of the time,
all the time...

Love me for better,
love me for worse,
but love me all of the time.

Every day I try to do better;
every day I get a little stronger,
especially when you're with me,

all of the time.

AlisRamie is from North Carolina, USA.

Interests include: philosophy, history, international relations, poetry, art, design, jazz, funk, and some good old soul.

Allpoetry.com/AlisRamie

[Mirza Lachinov]

The worst poet to be punished

You broke my wings as I had anticipated
However, I kept flying as I had said
The case is not the hurt in my wings I feel
It is - you even felt no difference of the result

You did not consider how far I could have flown
How high I could have soared if you let me keep on
It didn't even matter to you anything, maybe
You are right, who needs a strayed poet or poetry?!

It hurts to accept sometimes a scornful truth that
Poets are weird and also clay-brained
Meanwhile, they can set a universe from chaos,
But they can do it only when they are regarded

Who cares about my suffering and fluctuations?!
Who cares even if I cared about you?
I tried to kill the regret in your eyes I had given
But I see that regret has turned into humiliation

All poets are drifters, all have to be killed
And the one inside me worth dying the most
I give his death warrant to you to be fulfilled
I'd be glad if it changed the expression in your eyes

Mirza Lachinov is from The Republic of Azerbaijan.
He is also known as Mirza Lazim in native literature.
Currently working on the publication of his books 'Willow shade'
and 'Flying Fish'.
Allpoetry.com/Willow_shade

[Misha Jane Berry]

White Demon

And there you were
The white demon that caught my eye
We canoodled among the forests
And then told me you had to go

Altering my sanity as you whispered Goodbye
All the other girls, they play my role
Such a sad story told
You made me into such tragic art

———————————

M. Berry is located in Surrey, UK. I'm a Maine coon enthusiast and drink one too many americanos. I absolutely adore watching a good figure skating performance - anytime, anywhere! Allpoetry.com/M._Berry

[Katarina Anne]

Goodnight Universe

Lilac lullabies
Whisper sweet symphonies
To the skies of tomorrow
Tucking in all of our yesterdays
And kissing the moon goodnight
Unborn thoughts linger
Amongst a sea of
So many souls
Who will rise again with the sun
And dwell upon the earth as one

———————————

I am an aspiring poet from South Jersey. Poetry is pouring out of
me, and I have felt an affinity for words for as long as I can
remember. Allpoetry.com/KatarinaAnne

[Ina J Evans]

My prize, your flesh

I wear you like a signature scent
always carrying a smell of depravity
and, a touch of obsession

designed by your resistance
and your reservations

Your insistent need to keep me
at a distance only draws me
closer to your fold

I need to get you
caught under my hold

It makes me want to pull you closer
to hold on a little tighter
than I ever did before

I can't let me get away this time
I must have been out of my mind
you know you drive me
out of my mind

I like the way you fight
I don't care how hard you fight
I'll keep pushing until I tire you down

I didn't expect something
so precious to come so easily

when I know
I'll make my prize
your flesh

I never cared for an easy spread
I think it's better to pry it open
or it wouldn't be worth the time
to take to mount and, spread
You easy

I got plenty of time
to tire you down
I'll linger around and, wait
for however long it takes
to get under your skin

_____

From Atlanta GA, poetry is my art - I paint pictures with words.
I write poems instead of keeping a diary. They are my
confessions. I work as a massage therapist; I also sing and play
piano. Allpoetry.com/Ina_Evans

[Carlos Vargas]

Stardust

Your atoms are truly made out of stardust.

There are swirls of galaxies in the intricate design of your eyes and twice as many stars when they glimmer with jubilation.

The veins inside your body connect and collide like constellations, while synapses act as shooting stars as they race to bring you life.

Your mind is a supernova, exploding with a myriad of colors and bright new ideas, shining more brightly than the rest around you.

You create the gravity that makes me slowly drift towards you and you have become the black hole that devours me.

Your soul traveled light-years to find a home within your body and your love, like the universe, is constant and ever expanding.

The cosmos conspired to bring you here in this point and place in time so I can witness the art and beauty in the celestial being you are.

You may have been born on Earth, but your heart, body, and mind belong to the universe.

You're my universe.

I'm from Los Angeles, California. I'm a screenwriter, filmmaker, and a dreamer. Poetry always came as second nature to me, but I never fully explored it because I never had a muse. Until I met her. Allpoetry.com/Cheerupcharlie

[April Hamlin- Sache]

Angel

I'm looking at the sky while I walk
I see the stars and the moon
I think of my angel up above me

They say everyone has an angel that
watches over us, when it rains,
It's God's tears

But wait, hold up, I wanna talk to my angel
So I strike up this conversation every day, it's an ongoing thing

Good morning to my angel
Good evening to my angel
My angel has wings to fly away
I wish that I could fly away like my angel

――――――――――

April Hamlin- Sache is from Gary, Indiana. I love to write, it is
my therapy. Writing allows me to express my feelings and
experiences. It also allows me to create fiction.
Allpoetry.com/April_Sache

[Stephan V. Mastison]

Goddess

On the wings of our imagination. I travel through the night.
Suspended between heaven and earth.
Above us the endless night sky with a patchwork of countless stars
woven into it.
Beneath me the emerald sea.
As I move across the face of the water, my eyes scan the waves.
I can pierce the veil and see the goddess, her loving smile feels us
with hope and love and her outstretched arms call us home.

I smile and descend beneath the waves and return to her. I am at
peace, I am loved, and I am home.

––––––––––––––––

My name is Stephan V. Mastison and I am a published author
with two books, 'Shadows in the Mist' and 'Crossroads, and the
journey home'. My hope is to inspire and be thought provoking.
Allpoetry.com/Stephan_Mastison

[Saad Ali]

Immortality

Neitzsche proclaimed:
"God is dead!"

Alright, Neitzsche.
I do acknowledge your nihilistic-odyssey
to (reaching) the nirvana: nothing-ness.
Don't be so mad.

But you see,
'God' cannot really be dead-dead,
for it lives through its words.
Just as you aren't really dead-dead,
since thee live through thy discourses.
And my gratitude to you
for thy thoughts and words: knowledge.

The moral of the story is
true immortals are
the recorded and registered thoughts
id est words.
Your material and immaterial existence
can be annihilated.
But the words are the only beings
who can ever truly testify
to the everlasting flavours of elixir.
Hence, let your thoughts

transcend and manifest as words.
And do not resist it:
be bitten by words--
let their venom
render
all the cells in your blood
and all the neurons in your brain
mad.
id est elevate to the state
beyond the zenith of masochism.
id est achieve self-annihilation.
So that
you may
be rendered
immortal.

Saad Ali is from Lahore, Pakistan. id est means 'that is' or 'in other words'. He has lived (studied and worked) in the UK for almost a decade. He is a professional management and marketing consultant. His hobbies include: travelling & sports. Allpoetry.com/Saad_Ali

[Lisa F. Raines]

Quiet my fears, show me the lies

Please enlighten me with your wizened eyes
More mortal souls have lost their lives
On a summer's eve very like tonight

_____

AlisRamie is from North Carolina, USA.
Interests include: philosophy, history, international relations,
poetry, art, design, jazz, funk, and some good old soul.
Allpoetry.com/AlisRamie

[Phillip Davis]

CAW CAW, missing feather

What a dashing young pilot.
He is known for leaving the nest early saying but a couple words
of farewell.
Flying the straight and narrow,
from California to Delaware.
It takes just days in fact -
What a hero they would say,
What a spirit.
His armour and sword wouldn't let him feel much better than a
medium.
How does that work, he asks?
No reply.
But one
Only won
I
Your just my type of guy!

————————————

Title is from my love of my life Jill
My best writing is in the morning when reality is not set in of this
dimension.
Bio of my life would be too many. Books of twisted lives
Allpoetry.com/Phil36

[Lisa F. Raines]

The Stench of War

The hot breath of Death hangs in the air;
smelling of seared meat and acrid gunfire,
it invites me to retch and heave.

I try to avoid sticky pools of blood;
Horrific scenes in their reflection
haunt my every dream.

These days defy credulity—
poisoning my passions, numbing my heart
to the means of this Tragedy.

We may not need
to send soldiers to bleed,
returning them home Incomplete.

The day of the bleeding
machine is at hand,
but our Victory will not seem complete.

We all must embrace
the case for Peace
to defeat the warring Conceit.

AlisRamie is from North Carolina, USA.

Interests include: philosophy, history, international relations, poetry, art, design, jazz, funk, and some good old soul.

Allpoetry.com/AlisRamie

[Nitya Beriwal]
Theory of everything

Lost at the junction of life and consciousness,
being aware of complexity seems to be a beautiful predicament.
Colors and sounds create a mosaic trompe l'oeil,
as now euphoria is deciphered as a play of endorphins in the
mighty brain.

My mind searches for eternal tranquility,
while my brain reasons the crude reality.
The warmth of life is presently reduced to being a string of
photons,
and all human intricate feelings just to the chaotic firing of the
limbic masters in our control center.

I wonder at the simplex complexity and the Tao of life,
as I know all that awaits is a dance of fractals.
They dance to varying frequencies in an energy field,
as there is no color no sound only pure awareness dipped in
illusion.

Solidity and vanity are fueled by atomic vibrations,
while the serene colors of the sky are an amalgamation of diverse
wavelengths.
Life seems to be a maze, while my companion coffee causes
positive ionotropic effects,
and my sweet tooth spells the chant for my sweet dreams.

Well, I realize I live in a holographic universe,
with innumerable possibilities like the Schrödinger's cat.
Infinite things such as placebo still haunt our reasoning,
as we are akin to a robot in a Chinese room as what we know is an
iota in the sea of reality.

———————————

I am a passionate physician. I believe that poetry is the written language of emotions and ideas. For me, it is the abstract song of one's thoughts. Allpoetry.com/Nitya819

[Kristopher Burnett]

Broken

It's hard to truthfully say that I'll be alright
I've been traveling in this tunnel, and I don't see any light
My future's just dark now, but was once so bright
I pray all the time that I wake and things aren't what they seem
But every morning I wake, only to realize it's not a dream

I'm constantly searching for a way out of my personal hell
It's like my spirit is locked away and screaming to get out of its cell
Whether it is my broken body or my stagnate mind, I can't tell
I watch people advance through life, and I wish them well
But it seems like my life is that ship, floating without a sail

Until I was told not to dwell on the past
I never knew time goes by so fast
It gets pretty boring watching time just pass
I wanted to live free, as free as a fish in the ocean
Or as free as wild birds
So I figured it was time for a change
I'll write, and I'll live through my words

Kristopher Burnett is from Jackson, MS. Most of his writing is
his way of coping with a life altering tragedy.
Allpoetry.com/Krisburn

[Anna Mortis]

I've been gone a while

I've been gone a while, did you notice?
eternal wandering over the sixty-four squares
there is only black and white
nothing in-between.

I know now though
there are no other pieces
no way to draw a close
I find myself alone.

Within this endless longing
checkmate can never be
it's always about keeping others comfortable
Why must death be kept from me?

––––––––––––––––––

My untrained, saturnine ramblings sustain my life. I live in the
Northern Rivers district of New South Wales in Australia.
Allpoetry.com/Anna_Mortis

[Benita Hall]

Would You Have Regrets

If you suddenly opened your eyes and realized I was no longer
here.
That you didn't call more often just to say hey.
That you didn't see me more often.
That you didn't hug me more.
That you didn't share your secrets more.
That you didn't take the time to say I love and miss you.
That you couldn't see my smile.
That you couldn't hear my voice.
That you couldn't feel my touch.
That you couldn't smell my scent.
If you suddenly realized that there was so much you didn't say or
do.
Maybe because you felt it wasn't important.
Maybe you felt that you could say or do it later.

I ask myself the same question and sadly say yes.
Yes, I have so many regrets I can express now versus later.
I regret I spent more time focused on work and studying than
cherishing precious moments with you.
I regret demanding you be silent instead of listening when you
tried to give me an explanation.
I regret the responses I gave when you simply wanted to know
how my day was.
I regret pushing you away when you just wanted a hug, kiss, or
simply to cuddle with me.

182

I regret every game, conference, and appointment I missed.

I regret not spending time with you when you wanted me to due to my own selfish reasons.

Yes, I have too many regrets to put them down.

What I regret most is that I can't get the moments back as they're gone forever.

So much I would do different if I could just get the moments back.

But I can't get them back.

I can only cherish every moment I have with you now as tomorrow is promised to no one.

I can only express how much love and pride I have for you as often as it comes to mind so that you never forget or doubt it.

I want you to always remember you are, have been, and always will be my reason for existing.

I want you to know that even though I am not and may not always be with you in body, I will always be with you in spirit.

If there comes a time when you can't remember anything else I want you to remember the sound of my voice, the curve of my smile, and the glimmer in my eyes when I look at you.

Most importantly I want you to always remember I LOVE YOU more than life itself.

Poetry is my form of therapy. I enjoy expressing my thoughts through art. This particular poem was written as a dedication to my sons. I hope it touches you just as it did me as I was writing it. Allpoetry.com/Benitahall

[Juan Pablo Segovia]

A place in time

Oh, how I miss her
Death,
merciless, ruthless death,
took her from me.
It took her body,
her frail and helpless body
but not her soul,
her soul stayed with me
refusing to go,
she waits for me.
I can feel her presence, her warmth
At night we talk, drink and dance
until I can dance no more.
It is my imagination, I know that,
but somewhere in time there is a place
where there is no past, no present and no future
There, and for all eternity,
she gazes into my eyes
and holding my hands
tells me how much she loves me.

_____

Retired, live in U S, California. Emigrated from Cuba
I like to write poetry as past time and also gardening.
Have a beautiful grandson that also lives in California. Very
smart, like his mother Allpoetry.com/Juan_Pablo_Segov

184

[Marri Rouse]

Magic Sand

Lost in my thoughts and searching for faith,
My husband tried to help but I wanted some space,
He said lets go to the beach and forget all our worries,
Reluctant I went but planned to just hurry,
When we got there I wasn't expecting much,
Some water, some sand, a comforting touch,
To my amazement something took me off guard,
A huge shelter of logs, I thought "that must have been hard",
We explored around and inside this odd structure,
Then we cuddled inside as the waves got all flustered,
That black and brown sand must have been magic that day,
Because all of my sadness just melted away,
I found on that beach the faith I had lost,
I realized I had love and that meant the most.

Marri Rouse (A.K.A. Joi Roi) is from Green Bay, Wisconsin. I started poetry as an outlet after a severe mental breakdown. It helped tremendously with the support of my loved ones and Allpoetry.com! Allpoetry.com/Joi_Roi

[Lisa F. Raines]

He is my heart

Always beating
strong and true
Living life on the inside
We're changed forever

Now, racing thoughts
Palpitations
A chilling sweat breaks
over my skin

Betrayal?
Connivance?
Why do I wonder
about faithlessness?

The night goes on
disappointment arises
Why and where, my love
I need my heart!

When does fear start?
The first midnight
or too many after?
I jump at every sound.

My heart breaks
with every slow tick
I can't help but stare
There's no solace in it

Frightened now
Wondering everything
Wreck, coma, death?
Shot? Please, god, no!

What? Dead phone?
Again? Really?
Heart, be still and strong
Please come home

———————————

AlisRamie is from North Carolina, USA.
Interests include: philosophy, history, international relations,
poetry, art, design, jazz, funk, and some good old soul.
Allpoetry.com/AlisRamie

[Kristyan Wilson]

Is it or is it not Divine destiny

Your majesty, is it only a fantasy
Or is it truly Divine destiny
In all sanity, pulling between charity and family
Although I appreciate your generosity,
I'm beginning to feel the over intensity
Deciding between the two
Indulging in curiosity, some believed both are an necessity
The unknown fear, reaches so dear and near
Foreseeing the atmosphere with all its clarity It's still unclear
In good faith, should I volunteer and turn a deaf ear
When I sincerely want to hear
Believe me when I say I am so sincere
On this side of the hemisphere
The temple that has not be mark or known
Eventually should have known there would have been an pioneer
All secrets are meant to be exposed
The truth has to unfold
But who should discover the hidden treasure in the temple
It's not that quite simple
There are many barriers
Within this carrier
Only the few, the proud, indeed must be a true warrior
As the selection comes within the enemy lines
The peace that consumes the outer shield, in trusting that
everything will be just fine

Beginning to see the signs

Not knowing I was indeed spiritually blind

But because of the fact that I am in tune, I do not assume

In Security! Within the lines of charity verses family

So your majesty, is it only a fantasy

Or is it truly Divine destiny

I need to know in order to keep my sanity

I plea!

As you can plainly see

Because you are the only one who truly knows me

You have made me free

So your majesty, is it only a fantasy

Or is it truly Divine destiny

Kristyan Wilson. Born 1989 in Savannah, Ga and got her B.S in Healthcare Management from South University I love to write because it allows me to express myself without any limitation. Allpoetry.com/Kristyan_Wilson

[Michael Cruce]

Peace for us, Peace For life, Peace for all,

Peace for love

Times are in shambles right now, with lots of crazy stuff going on. So crazy that its fuzzy, to even think about. How are we supposed to keep peace, when we don't hear a peep from people in beyond. They ignore, and ignore, it's so poor. That could also be why we are in sorrow at the moment. Violence is overboard, but lots of times they are silent, because they believe that if you're silent about it, violence will become silence.

How can we keep positive things in pair, when it seems like that part of it is attacked by a bear? Of course not everything is attacked, but it's still not fair that folks in beyond just doesn't care. There are some places in earth that's just as sweet as a pear still.

I don't need to take a pill to fill in the gaps, no I don't dare to do that, not at all, because sweetness is still there, but sourness, seems to be evolving from powerless, to powerful. I can't believe we just sit here and let it happen. What we need is a captain to lead us, and life to the peace we are known to have. The bears are running loose, but lots of people in the beyond still just don't care. However, what they need to know is that we are not going to live in fear, because it's not fair for them to think that we are under it all.

What we need is peace for us, peace for life, peace for all, and peace for love. The doves are flying in the world still living life, fairly, and of course they just love it all, especially when we call them doves, love doves, love doves they want to us to think. Just because a dove is a bird, it doesn't mean they don't know how to love. We need to be like them. Love your doves, love your life, and bring peace for us, for life, for all, and for love. Right now, the world needs more of that.

The world is in shambles, and we can hear rambles all around us, daily. So next time you see a dove, think love, think peace, think peace for all, and peace for us. Because again the world needs peace for us, peace for life, peace for all, and peace for love. It's time we start waking up to the rambles all around us.
Peace for us, Peace for life, Peace for all, and peace for love is what we need. Stop the bear outbreak, because right now many things aren't so fair. What we need is more sweet pears in the world. The world needs more sweetness like a pear.

———————————

Hello my name is Michael Cruce, I have been writing poems and stories since I was a kid. I am 27 now, and I live in Marietta, Georgia USA. I am trying to make my writings known more. Allpoetry.com/Michael_Cruce

[Lenard Carter]

In the Final Hour

Although perplexed against the strong winds blowing
a kind of chaos that sustains the fabric of life
here I stand at the white cliffs of Dover
I'm sitting on a big rock up high on the grass
looking into thine own life that is nearly over
my seafaring forefathers traveled these oceans
here the ancestral change runs a mixed emotion
this moment takes time to nourish
after caring for and nurturing
my eccentric old man
and his will that became frail with dementia
'twas the least I could do

Previously I traveled the world to some end
exploring the language culture and ale
now I observe the many years that have transpired
juxtaposed against a higher conscience
in history the waters ran the rage
turning in what occurred at sea
those who fought in 20th century wars
built a legacy and freedom for the people
like my grandfather Sergeant John Carter
in the 1914 frontier clash at the Battle of Mons
a victory at overwhelming odds
and mine own father in the merchant navy
seeing war up close the first time

crossing the Atlantic Ocean
bombed, torpedoed and run ashore
many a time they witnessed bloodshed
yet brave, patriotic and proud
to serve under his majesty
King George the V and VI
remarkably this notion was widespread

Making their way in the MV Lambrook
with Captain Kennedy to Bari 1943
my father the captain's tiger
and all his shipmates
witnessed many lives lost that day
yet for them luck would have its way
as they prayed in silence
they lived to tell their tales
throughout the long hard years askew
eventually they did marry
the women raised many a fine young fellow
and charming delightful bearers
hence although time had made them weary
they comforted me in my youth
and although they suffered
that which had clearly required of them
a passage to the hard truth
they renounced their fears
throughout the whole ordeal
and still they comforted me in my youth

Here in the beautiful panoramic countryside
one more shipwreck comes to rest its bow
in the final hour its spirit begins the epic journey
like a wayward son off to join a collective army
on the mend now in the awakening
flying over the chasm of broken hearts
an uncle from a post-war family sadly departing
at the end of this line we are grateful and all
his spirit prepares to transcend
and help thee mend joining the others in afterlife
born of a classic noble-blood
lost but not forgotten
it is here that we stand for divided we fall
like the wall in Joshua fit the battle of Jericho
and the Onedin Line where the wind blew free
for the last in line walls come tumbling down
if it were not for a man and his travels
who created a large loving family
yet time passes a clan with sorrow-love
stories unfold for those left behind
established tales of yesteryear
from Beerwolf's inventive scholar
for the young from the old
a nostalgic breath
one more story is told

With eyes ready to read the faith
that flies in the light winds across earth
winds that slowly blew out

once strong and happy energised flames
we make way for late arrivals in the nick of time
setting alight and igniting anew
those little lives given new names
from the DNA an inheritance
of all that has come before
relinquished and bequeathed
for all that will go beyond
we must make room
and comfort the quench for thirst
'tis in this context we accept the great knowledge
passed down into our hands century twofold
an inner wisdom with the nature of good standing
richness comes from hard work beforehand
what has become
crossing this mighty sea
in the hands of a god
who does not forsake thee

We are grateful for what has been
surely I can speak for all others that see
and those that do not shine of immortality
bring forth joy to those hearts we harbour
resting on shoulders of mortal reality
naturally with great sadness lives are lost
the sprinkling sea salt spits at my head again
I pray: It's to God the Holy Spirit we turn
where ships have run ashore
submerged and tumbled

the sea has been tried and tested
many years on end
I can hear the eerie silence
and the slow creaking rumble
of those lives and ships lost at sea in battle misery
and others who were traveling to the promise land
meeting the unforgiving wrath of the mighty waters
others fit for freedom and the right to prosperity
all that came to rest beneath thee
a bravery unmatched by modern travelers

As I stand here and bequeath a promise kept
carry on the peaceful works when I hit the dirt
perhaps some living connected lives will hurt
and others that may not
like the spurting and the churning
of these unforgiving waves
hitting up against each other
there's many a nautical mile to travel
unravel what has come to be
and without a question of doubt
in the end unequivocally
we begin to see
where we have been
what we have done
and where we stand
with these thoughts in mind
I wave my hand
farewell father let it be

but before I can drop my arm
down toward the ground
I search the sea
and my eyes connect
with an objective reality

Ahoy there! What's this?
what looks like a lonely bottle
approaching floating across the sea
bopping up bopping down
perhaps this is a maiden voyage
slowly it edges closer to the shoreline cliffs
and comes to rest within the shallow salty water
there must be a message in tow
arriving for the one at last
I walk down the track to get a closer view
I make my way through the valley hillside
the side of the chasm where sea meets land
the bottle keeps drifting toward me like a magnet
I slide and clamber down the rest excitedly
believing it must be meant for thee
a message in a bottle
but before I get the chance to hold said
it crashes on a rock and the cork pops open
the weary papered message kept safe and dry
falls to the white sandy ground of Dover
and enters the environment around
I carefully lift it up
preparing to be honoured with the moment

astonishingly marveled
and thankful for the read:
"Signs are laid out in the pathway ahead
choose the right path as you walk through
the valley of the shadow of death
fear no evil
when you set out
to accomplish a task
in order that you shall break
and eat from the bread of life-
and all the children say, amen!"

After all is said and done
the seven seas linger on
lighthouses will stand strong
to guide thee
much longer after we are gone
the trumpets sound
like a fanfare for common man/women
I awake from the momentum of truth
I look around and come to realize that
although some walls may crumble and fall
life is transferred to the living to do the giving
the waters gather past life connections
and the shifting of the sand moves them
to a place of new beginnings
back and forth with the moon's bulging tides
the beat goes on long after we are gone
so fear not my friend there is life after death

Len began writing at the age of 12. Born in NZ and originating from Cumbria, he feels connected to the Lake Poets, they did not follow any stringent school of thought or literary practice. Dedicated to my family line and all those who fought for freedom. Allpoetry.com/Anəmɪlɔdʒka

[Juan Pablo Segovia]

An old friend

He was a true friend, a faithful friend,
more than family, more than a brother,
a friend without questions, a friend without conditions.
He was a gentle man with a heart of gold.
I will never forget

Years have passed
in an instant,
now only memories

Life took us on different paths.
Where did he go?
What became of him?
Did he change?
Will he still be my friend?
Not like before, I know that,
we are not the same
time changed us
Little by little, it stole what we were.

Memories of joy,
memories of hope,
memories of sadness,
memories of fear,
adventure memories,
memories of mischief.

Memories darken,
memories of times gone by
that won't come back
Times I love.
My thoughts fly aimlessly
searching, searching,
lost in time.
With a smile, I remember

————————————

Retired, I live in California, USA. Emigrated from Cuba
I like to write poetry as past time and also garden.
I have a beautiful grandson that also lives in California – he is very
smart, like his mother. This is dedicated to Raulise, my eternal
friend. It was a privilege and honor that you were a part of my life.
Allpoetry.com/Juan_Pablo_Segov

[Lisa F. Raines]

Foolosophy

Some "Big" men
call others
"Boy", and worse.

Is it so
they can feel
like "real" men?

This must be
a fleeting
sensation!

———————————

AlisRamie is from North Carolina, USA.
Interests include: philosophy, history, international relations,
poetry, art, design, jazz, funk, and some good old soul.
Allpoetry.com/AlisRamie

[Juan Pablo Segovia]

A fallen tree

She loved her fig tree,
I believe it loved her too

In the mornings she would rush to it and eat the fruit,
she knew that the birds would try to get there first.
The tree was young, strong and healthy,
she was not

Her final days were painful and agonizing
The tree felt her pain,
one night it broke in two and fell,
the branches leaned against her room and slowly died

Why did the tree die?
Did it die of sadness?

––––––––––––––––––

Retired, live in U S, California. Emigrated from Cuba
I like to write poetry as past time and also gardening.
Have a beautiful grandson that also lives in California. Very
smart, like his mother Allpoetry.com/Juan_Pablo_Segov

[Robert Scott Henry]

Repeat

Close your eyes and listen in
I'll whisper my lies with a grotesque grin
And while truth dies, I'll spin and spin
And play upon your fear within.

Repeat, repeat and keep alive
The sweetest myths and let them thrive
The words will ooze and bleed and spread
And drip upon your callow head.

Close your eyes and listen in
I'll whisper my lies with a grotesque grin
And while truth dies, I'll spin and spin
And play upon your fear within.

Ignore, dismiss consistency
Amend, rewrite our history
Who needs findings, figures, facts
When there are more desired tracks.

Repeat, repeat and keep alive
The sweetest myths and let them thrive
The words will ooze and spread and bleed
And pour upon your want and greed.

Repeat, repeat and keep alive
The sweetest myths and let them thrive
The words will bleed and spread and ooze
And flood your thoughts and bleakest views.

Close your eyes and listen in
I'll whisper my lies with a grotesque grin
And while truth dies, I'll spin and spin
And play upon your fear within.
Repeat, repeat, repeat.

Robert Scott is an award winning British playwright. His scripts range from dark tragedies to light comedies and have currently been performed around the world. Allpoetry.com/Robert_Scott

[Alex Crowcroft]

The Enlightened State Of Mind

Enlightened, what up?
Its my only state of being
Relative to my mind, sprouts the buds of a treeling
It's our physical state, embracing your soul
Inhale deep, consciousness in my bowl
It's all but a dream, realistic hallucinations
Projecting the truth, it's soul powered elation
This canvas called earth, it'll rattle your brain
An unknown epiphany leaves us all insane
For better, for worse, It makes you wonder
Don't take life for granted, a celestial blunder
Experience space, elevate, time to give
Playful, insightful, its bomb ya dig?

So take a look through the glass, proverbial in size
It's a sliver of a footprint, microscopic, alive
As I sit here in wonder, exploration I find
These questions I ponder, keep flowing, a ride
Concentration ensues, each stroke, yeah its brilliance
Infinitely described, poetic resilience
The time, yeah we mold it, shapes who we are
The path that I've chosen, leads to the stars
It ends, an explosion, we cease to exist
This plane, yes, we travel, lively in bliss
It's my consciousness a light, that's creative stride
Like jesus on the cross, no way I'll abide

Comprehension, the dawn, our minds become free
Follow me kindly, scale my mind, simply be.

Alex Crow which translates to his pen name Ec Warlox, only ever
has control of the first few words he writes in any piece. After that
there is a disconnect and the creative muse takes the helm.
Allpoetry.com/Ec_Warlox

[Jack L. Martin]

Sit Down, Shut Up and Listen!

You all have controlled my whole life
as if you were all on a mission
now it's your turn to learn of my concern
so, sit down, shut up and listen!

You thought you knew what was best for me
you thought that the police would have arrested me
you watched as my peers all beat up on me
But you never asked ME what was best for me!

You chose a life for me that's the hardest
you know I just wanted to be a good artist
my life would have been meager and honest
for years I ended up on the con list

If you just would have opened your eyes
you all would have watched me glisten
instead of pushing all those lies and surprise
now please, sit down shut up and listen!

Straight from school I enrolled in the ARMY
Desert Storm put a lot of bad harm on me
though it made me a strong man of harmony
It feels like I had a lobotomy!

I thought I wanted to be a rock star
all the alcohol and fun drugs were not far
I spent most of my nights at the corner bar
my body and my life filling up with tar

If you just would have opened your mind
you would have noticed that I was on a mission
now it is time for the blind to be kind
Will you please just shut up and listen?

All of my mentors have died
no one around for me to blame
watch as my life starts to slide
down the gutter, what a crazy ride!

I struggle but still I stay tame
I have the world, but nothing to gain
yet somehow I deal with the pain
I wonder how people stay sane?

I finally turned things around
married a good woman who keeps me on the ground
I stay focused and listen to the sound
of life's path that that has yet to be found

I'm finally found peace with my life
I ignored all your critique and dissin'
You would all be where I am today
If you would of just shut up and listened!

[Kathryn Alley]

Beyond the Pale

Was the summer I turned fifteen,
when somehow things went wrong.
I heard it on the wind
and in the night bird's song

The world went on the same,
as the days they always do.
I ran from learning things,
that could tear a soul in two

I watched in fascination,
as they laid her on the slab.
Her eyes no longer sparkling,
her dress, a rusty drab

Her skin so alabaster,
once warm, now cold to touch
They made me sit there by her,
this one I loved so much

When darkness drew her curtain,
and the candle burned too low,
she rose, this I was certain,
as my fear bade me to go

But I heard all, as she told me,
that I was sleepin' sound.
I needed close to listen;
'fore they put her in the ground

She spoke of red haired Martin,
said that he had had his way,
and to keep from Papa knowin';
well, he put her where she lay

She told me rectify this
Make sure that devil paid,
then smiled, and touched my cheek,
as still, on the slab, she laid

No one knows what happens,
when the night fades into blue,
'Cause the grave they were a diggin'
went from one, then numbered two

See Martin was a sleepin',
in the room just off of mine,
and my hair spike, somehow managed,
his gray matter there to find

He comes and sees me sometimes,
To ask me how I'd known.
I just smile and walk away...
It's too close to the bone

Kat Alley is from a small town in West Virginia, currently living in Pa. She is currently loving the moment and grateful for all that it brings. Namaste. Allpoetry.com/Kat_Alley

[Arlice W. Davenport]
Anguish

(After Sartre)

There's a sorrow that overcomes us all.
There's a sickness that never can be healed.
Within itself, existence casts a pall
That no one can remove; the cover's sealed
Into the searing consciousness of all.
Its attributes can never be repealed.
They inform freedom, forcing us to call
For a meaning and value we can feel.
Death makes the veil of nothingness to fall
Over all the choices with which we deal.
We can't escape this burden or forestall
Making ourselves the judges of what's real.
It's a problem that suffocates us all:
We *solely* pick the cards that we must deal.

––––––––––––––––––

When I first started studying philosophy, I read Sartre and Plato
in a high school humanities class. Although I have a love-hate
relationship with him, I'm still fascinated by many of Sartre's
ideas. Allpoetry.com/arliced

[Laura Gallagher]

Liberate Yourself

Saddness is a crippling emotion
It sends you on a downward spiral
Suffocating you till you no longer function
Lost in a world of denial

Freedom of speech is hard, when words escape your mind
Fear of exposing oneself to disregard
Seeking Solace is difficult to find

With this cross we bear,
Our internal struggle will prevail
Rid of feelings that create despair
Shine your light and you will not fail

We all search for answers;
An inquisitive mind is healthy
Our inner happiness is all that matters
Live the life you were given and be free

_____

Hello, I am Laura, from the west of Ireland. Poetry for me is a great way to clarify feelings and put meaning to them. My poems are journeys taken and are filled with an overall message of love and light Allpoetry.com/LauraGall

[Marielle Diala]

Sought after

He called me sought after
When I was running away with my helicopter
He was chasing after me
But I was too blind to see
When I was running after my lover
He told me I am a person he can't get over
When I finally realized that I wasn't loved
He came to me and treated me like a dove
He called me sought after
I don't understand why
He keeps calling me a name that is unknown
So all I can do is cry
Because he addresses me to a name that
I cannot own
He called me sought after
I finally had the courage to ask him
He then brought me to a place where I would be fine
So I can hear him
Say you are mine
After hearing these words
I fell down on my knees
Because his words hurts
Like arrows shot in front of me
Tears fall down from my face
Because all these time I believed in lies

Still he gave me a place
Where people has the opportunity to rise
He called me sought after
My name is sought after
Because of my lover
Through him I can make the broken people laugh
And people who are in places that are rough
I will no longer wander
For my lover put a name on me
And I will forever be free
For he called me sought after.

BlueJade is currently living in New York City. Likes to play video games, watch anime and movies, read fiction books, and hanging out in dessert bars and coffee shops. She travels once a year. Allpoetry.com/BlueJade

[Rhonda Barringer]

Grandparents

Grandparents are special people we have,
they are not picked or specially made for us,
They are out there waiting and loving
the idea of being a grandparent.

If you are a parent,
You know the time will come when you
will become a grandma or grandpa.

You won't be ready to be one,
No one is,
But once it happens, you will enjoy it.

You will be able to do the spoiling, have fun,
and tell stories.
Then send them back to their parents,
nice and wired,
Just like everyone did to your kids.

There are no rules in your house,
Gramms & Gramps are your names,
and spoiling is your game.

Grandkids make grandparents
feel like kids themselves,

These are the moments that
they won't forget.

My name is Rhonda Barringer.
I work as a CSR Logistics Broker. I work with truck drivers that
pick up and deliver products all over the US. I have two children
& 2 grandchildren. Allpoetry.com/Writesolstice52

[Peter Witt]

Notes from Cell Wall

He passed his days
reading notes penned
by those gone before

No man knows my story
yet all sit in judgment

They can pen my soul
but the final chapter
has yet to be written

I miss her sad eyes
pleading with me
to remember I am loved

I sinned against God
and my wife
God will forgive me

Whoever reads this
know you are not alone

No walls, nor bars
can contain the human spirit

Write something ironic,
I'll be back to read it soon

Reading notes of hope and shame
he crushed a cockroach
and wrote in ichor:

I pass among you
humbled and unbowed

_____

Peter Witt lives in Bryan, TX. Took up writing poetry in 2018.
Also researches and writes about family history.
Allpoetry.com/Oakblue34

[Michelle R Sass]

Emotions

My heart hurts
my head is confused
My emotions are lost
You did what I thought you never would
Here we are
Standing as 2 separate people
No longer as 1
My heart hurts
I feel so empty
So lost
So out of control of what's around me
I didn't sleep much
I toss and turn
Every little thing startled me
You say you're sorry
Say you'll never do it again
But will you?
Will you get angry again?
Will I be the one it's taken out on again?
I have all of these questions
And no answers out of fear
How do we go on from here?
Where do we start
Will this be the end of us?
I guess only time will tell

Just a small town girl from Scapppoose OR, that uses poetry as a way to deal with emotional turmoil.
Allpoetry.com/Michelle_Sass

[Lisa F. Raines]

You Disappointed Me Today

You used to be happy
What happened to that?

You used to have fun
Now you have none

You used to joke and tease
Now nothing will please

You used to whistle happily
Now you treat us crappily

This is not a you
I ever wanted to see.

What is happening
to my family?

Who are you, always mad
You took away my Dad

_____

AlisRamie is from North Carolina, USA.
Interests include: philosophy, history, international relations,
poetry, art, design, jazz, funk, and some good old soul.
Allpoetry.com/AlisRamie

[Rebecca Brodzenski]
You choke on pysch pills

Been diagnosed
with agoraphobia
definition described
a hermit who can't trust

Back then I was young n dumb
thought I found true love
only found love makes you numb

Ate fucking psycho meds
till I couldn't leave bed

I was almost convinced this wrong
you twisted love so you could sneak
I caught you stealing my strong
ends up YOU who is weak

Almost had me, I almost didn't see
you should have moved on
you lost when you chose me
my strength (it turns out) is too strong

I don't hate you, I'm not even mad
I've been nothing but real
love, I need not use
to steal

In fact, I'm quite glad
my weakness you stole instead
YOU gained it
that part of me you can have!

My name is Rebecca Brodzenski. I'm from Sebring, Ohio. I am 37 years old and I have 5 children and one grandchild. Poetry has been my way of releasing what's on my mind and I'm grateful to God for it Allpoetry.com/Rebecca_Brodzens

[Lindsey Johnson]
No Longer Dependent

Until the day I met you
I did not know what it meant to fall in love.
We fell in love fast and hard
Promising to spend our lives in each other's arms

It was not until the day we parted
I realized I am stronger than I thought

Thank you for making me realize
I am capable
I am strong
And,
I am independent

––––––––––––––––––

Lindsey Johnson is a current business student. In her spare time she enjoys reading science fiction with her cats and drinking tea.
Allpoetry.com/Johns297_myumani

[Patricia LeDuc]

Another Time, Another Place

When you put your hand upon my face
I was transported to a safe place
It helped me come to realize
I had so much pain to erase
But I wasn't alone...
I drew strength from your touch
Your kindness meant so much
It came from your heart
And went straight to my soul
Making a connection showing me how
To win back my life
To take back control
But I didn't miss
The wistful look in your eyes
It came as no surprise
As if to say
Another time
Another place
Your hand upon my face
No pain to erase
Wondering
What might have been

Poetry is a creative way to clear my mind and put my thoughts into words. Mother/Grandmother/Happily Retired. I live in Middletown, Connecticut Allpoetry.com/Patricia_LeDuc

[Jenny Linsel]

The Birthday Party

Early friday morning an envelope
Dropped onto Edith's welcome mat
Inside was a Birthday Party Invite
Adorned by a picture of a Siamese cat

The party was to celebrate the birthday
Of Edith's old nemesis, Mary
They'd never really got on
So the invite made her quite wary

Edith recognised the hand-writing
Of Mary's daughter Jill
Who had often taken time off work
To look after her mother when she was ill

The party was on monday night
At the local social club
Edith couldn't understand why that was the venue
When Mary's son ran his own pub

Then she suddenly remembered
Rumours of a family feud
Something about money loaned but never paid back
Had prompted Mary's Will to be renewed

Edith knew that Mary's other daughter Kim
Wouldn't be invited to the party
Because Mary was ashamed of her
For dressing cheap and tarty

Suddenly the phone rang
It was Mary's daughter Jill
She said "Are you coming to Mum's party?
She really hopes you will"

Edith was lost for words
Then mumbled "We've never seen eye to eye"
Jill shocked Edith to the core
Saying "Mum wants to say her last goodbye.

She's terminally ill
and hasn't got long left.
If you don't go to her party
she will be bereft"

Edith said that she would go
If it meant so much to her mother
She didn't dare to ask about
Jill's sister and her brother

On the morning of the party
Edith didn't know what to wear
But as long as she turned up
Mary wouldn't really care

When Edith arrived at Mary's party
Jill took her to one side
She said "I need to speak to you about mum,
Before we go inside.

Mum was shocked when I said you were coming
After all the bad blood in the past
She wants to call a truce
Now she's on her last"

Edith gave Jill a hug and said
"I'm glad we can make amends,
But it shouldn't take something like this
To make us realise our true friends"

Edith and Jill went into the party
And Mary was the centre of attention
There were so many guests
They'd filtered out into the extension

Mary was seated at the head table
Downing a glass of brown ale
The first thing Edith noticed
Was that she suddenly looked so frail

Mary placed her present on the table
Then read the nice verse in Edith's card
She said "I know we haven't got on in the past
Coming here must have been very hard"

Edith said she'd wanted to come
There was nothing she'd rather do
Mary could tell from Edith's expression
Of her illness she already knew

The icing on the cake had begun to melt
It had been on the table for hours
It was a handbag made of fondant
Filled with edible flowers

Someone suggested Mary should blow out the candles
But that was a huge mistake
She pursed her lips, blew and her dentures flew out
Then landed upon the cake

Everyone burst out laughing
And Mary was wearing a big grin
She calmly picked up her dentures
And put them straight back in

Reverend Smith ate peanuts from Mary's plate
And said they were simply the best
Mary told him that once she'd sucked off the chocolate
She had to leave the rest

The party was a great success
And when Mary had said her goodbyes
She looked at Edith who'd stayed behind
With a wistful look in her eyes

"I'm so glad that you came
And that we've made amends
If I hadn't been so judgemental
We could have been really good friends"

Mary took a sip of whiskey
From a small monogrammed flask
And Edith told her if she needed anything
She only had to ask

Jill told Edith her car was outside
And if she needed a lift home she would take her
Mary said "Goodbye, dear friend
Soon I'll be off to meet my maker"

Edith was lost for words
And felt a tear run down her cheek
Then said that they should meet for coffee
Maybe sometime next week

Jill drove Edith home
And thanked her for being so nice
Edith thought she'd repay her
By giving her some good advice

"Try not to bear grudges
If you can make amends, don't wait
Because one day you'll discover
You've left it far too late"

I am from Hartlepool in the United Kingdom. I write poetry because I find it very cathartic. My poems are usually about things I remember from my past. Allpoetry.com/Jenruff2001

235

[Lisa F. Raines]

Headphones, really?

We used to love the music
filling the house.

We sang, danced, and
joked around together.

Now we're banished to
headphones and earbuds.

You know, the kids are
awfully quiet these days.

Music's a social lubricant,
but now has become a reason,
even a cause, for isolation.

In sharing what we hear,
and see, and feel,

It makes us build our world,
our community,
together,

remember?

AlisRamie is from North Carolina, USA.

Interests include: philosophy, history, international relations, poetry, art, design, jazz, funk, and some good old soul.

Allpoetry.com/AlisRamie

Made in the USA
Middletown, DE
14 January 2020